THE
GULF ISLANDS
EXPLORER
THE•OUTDOOR•GUIDE

THE
GULF ISLANDS
EXPLORER
THE • OUTDOOR • GUIDE

Bruce Obee

WHITECAP BOOKS
Vancouver/Toronto

Cover photographs by Bob Herger
All other photographs, except those on pages 28 and 199,
by Bruce Obee
Photographs on pages 28 and 199 by Janet Barwell-Clarke

Chapter head drawings by Suzanne Gagnon, Ganges, B.C.
Maps by Janet Barwell-Clarke, Deep Cove, B.C.
Typography by CompuType, Vancouver, B.C.
Printed and bound in Canada by Friesen Printers, Altona, Manitoba

Canadian Cataloguing in Publication Data

Obee, Bruce, 1951-
    The Gulf Islands Explorer

    ISBN 0-895099-21-8

    1. Gulf Islands (B.C.) — Description and travel — Guide-books.
    I. Title.
FC3845.G8A3 1990   917.11′28   C90-091169-7
F1089.G8O23 1990

    First Edition 1981
    Second Printing 1984
    Third Printing 1985
    Fourth Printing 1988
    Second Edition 1990

Published by
Whitecap Books
1086 West 3rd Street
North Vancouver, B.C.
V7P 3J6

BY THE SAME AUTHOR
The Pacific Rim Explorer — The Outdoor Guide

For my grandmother, Hilda Merriman:
a journalist's wife, a journalist's mother,
a journalist's grandmother,
an immeasurable influence.

C O N T E N T S

Chapter Three:
The Pender Islands —
Bays and Beaches 101

Chapter Four:
Galiano Island — An Island
That Leaves an Indelible Impression 119

Chapter Seven:
Gulf Islands Marine Parks —

THANKS TO ...

My wife Janet and daughters Nicole and Lauren for taking
me to the Gulf Islands ... my parents Bob and Joy Obee
for taking me there first ... my brothers Les and Eric for
defining "skunked" ... George Robinson for his patience,
posing and unsolicited advice ... Deb George, and Bruce
and Geoffrey Smith, Jim Rodgers and Devon Featherstone,
Capt. David Betts ... famous fishermen Jim Gilbert and
Charlie White ... Slippery Vic Talson for redefining
"skunked' ... hikers Roy and Ann Kingerlee, and Dana
Dahlquist and Jo Axe ... canoeists Sharon Bartlett, Jim
Morris, Liz Hughes, Doug Rushton, Lauren One and Sam
... Linda and Laura Whitney, David and Sara Tasker,
Kirsten Bristow, David May, Bruce Bartle, Grant Cameron,
Joan Richardt, Gordon Cooper ... Mike and Allison
Lafortune for their neighbourliness ... and my uncle, Alec
Merriman, for his outdoors ethics and journalistic
curmudgeonry.

I N T R O D U C T I O N

When I was a youngster a friend of my father took our family to Galiano Island on his boat. We cruised out of Sidney past the ferries at Swartz Bay, along the southern shore of Saltspring and up Trincomali Channel to Montague Harbour. By the end of the day my father had made up his mind to buy a boat, a decision eagerly supported by his family. We had been captivated, all of us, by the magic of the Gulf Islands.

We spent our summers on the sea, cruising the islands, combing the beaches and hiking the woodlands that surrounded the sheltered nooks and harbours where we dropped anchor. The more I saw, the more I wanted to see: I became increasingly curious about the Gulf Islands, about the people who lived on them and the places we couldn't reach by boat.

As I began to explore the Gulf Islands by canoe, bicycle, ferry and car, I developed an insatiable thirst for more knowledge of the islands. I bought my own boat, subscribed to the *Gulf Islands Driftwood*, purchased books, nautical charts, topographic maps, and collected any information I could find on the Gulf Islands. This book is a compilation of facts and ideas I've gathered in trying to satisfy my curiosity about the Gulf Islands.

Since its original publication in 1981, one noticeable change around the Gulf Islands is an increasing number of kayakers. To accommodate these paddlers, I've added a new chapter on marine parks; now *The Gulf Islands Explorer* covers all of the marine parks in the southern islands.

Surprisingly little else has changed on the Gulf Islands in nearly a decade. When I returned to research this new, revised edition I found that populations have grown, businesses have come and gone, buildings have been built. But the outdoors, the gist of this book — the parks, the hiking trails, the cycling routes, the canoeing waters, the fishing spots, the diving depths, the beaches ... and the magic — is still much the same.

Deep Cove, Saanich Peninsula, B.C.   *Bruce Obee*
March, 1990

The Gulf Islands

A Place for People,
a Place for Solitude

 Snuggled against the southeast shores of Vancouver Island, the Gulf Islands lie sheltered from the infamous rains and blustery winds that blow from the open Pacific. Some 200 of these enchanting islands and islets are clustered on the leeward side of Vancouver Island, where the grassy woodlands and tranquil waters bear little resemblance to the dense rain forests and swollen seas of Vancouver Island's west coast. The mild, Mediterranean-type climate of Georgia Strait, between Vancouver Island and British Columbia's lower mainland, is so agreeable, in fact, that cactus grows in isolated patches on some of the southern islands.

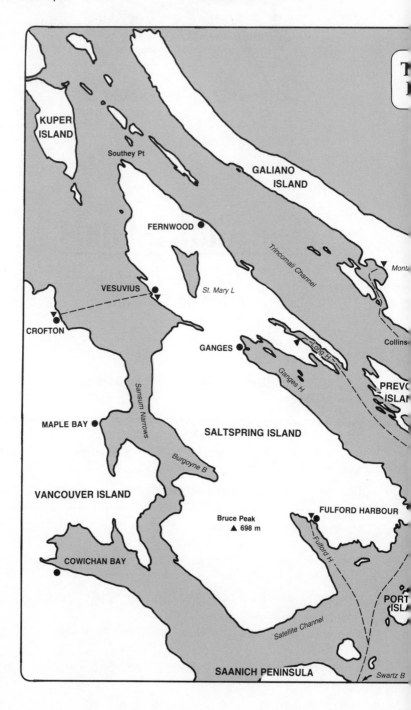

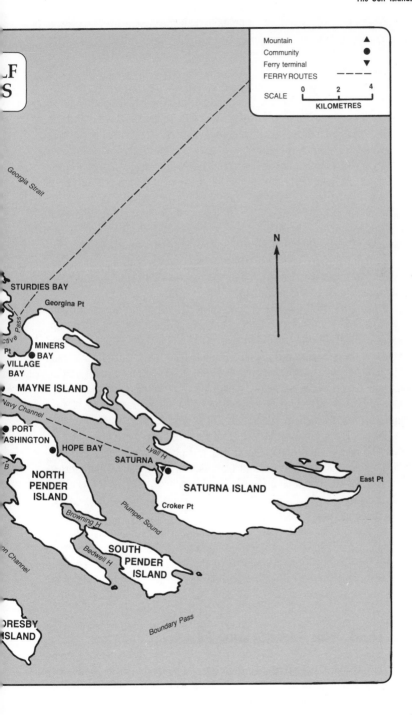

GULF
IS

Mountain ▲
Community ●
Ferry terminal ▼
FERRY ROUTES ------
SCALE
0   2   4
KILOMETRES

Georgia Strait

N

STURDIES BAY

Georgina Pt

Active Pass

Pt
MINERS
BAY
VILLAGE
BAY

MAYNE ISLAND

Navy Channel

PORT
WASHINGTON
HOPE BAY

Lyall H

SATURNA

B

NORTH
PENDER
ISLAND

SATURNA ISLAND

East Pt

Croker Pt

Browning H

Plumper Sound

on Channel

Bedwell H

SOUTH
PENDER
ISLAND

Boundary Pass

DRESBY
ISLAND

Most of the Gulf Islands are uninhabited and accessible only by private boat. The myriad coves and channels are travelled year-round by pleasure boaters, many of whom consider the waters of the Gulf Islands the finest cruising region in the world. But exploring the scenic beaches and forests of the Gulf Islands is not a privilege reserved exclusively for the wealthy yachtsman. The populated islands — Saltspring, North and South Pender, Galiano, Mayne and Saturna — are linked with Vancouver Island and the lower mainland by a fleet of government-operated car and passenger ferries. The vessels are an integral part of day-to-day life for many Gulf Islanders.

Foot passengers aboard ferries from Vancouver Island can pack a lunch and take a day-trip to a number of islands. For an additional fare they can take a car and spend some time touring the islands, returning to Vancouver Island the same day or staying overnight at a resort or campground on an island. Ferries travel inter-island after leaving the Vancouver Island terminal at Swartz Bay, 40 kilometres north of Victoria.

A similar day-cruise can be taken from Tsawwassen, 40 kilometres south of Vancouver. Ferries travel daily across Georgia Strait, through the islands, and back to the mainland in the evening.

Cruising the Gulf Islands by ferry provides a unique opportunity to view some of Canada's most magnificent scenery, taste the fragrant ocean air, and photograph the prolific marine life of the islands. The view from the decks of a ferry, however, is only a glimpse of the beauty throughout the islands. Farther inland there are sea-level valleys of pastoral farmland, spectacular panoramic seascapes seen from 700-metre mountain peaks, forests of towering Douglas fir and twisted arbutus trees, and placid, fly-fishing lakes stocked with smallmouth bass and fighting rainbow trout.

Many of the permanent islanders are retirees who have given up the bustle and confusion of big cities to live in a place conveniently close to civilization, yet comfortably distant from downtown. In tiny communities such as Port Washington on North Pender, Miners Bay on Mayne, or Montague Harbour on Galiano there is an aura of maritime hospitality, the kind found only on islands.

The Gulf Islands are a place for outdoors activities — hiking, canoeing, beachcombing or simply sipping something cool on the porch of a waterfront cottage. The forms of outdoor entertainment are as varied as the islands themselves and travellers can spend one day visiting four islands or a lifetime on one island.

The Land, the Forests and Fauna

There is no question that it is the scenery which attracts visitors from all over the world to the Gulf Islands. There are few places where you can sit quietly on a sheltered beach and enjoy an intimate view of a nearby rocky point, possibly with a solitary arbutus tree perched upon the end, yet where moving only a few metres from the same sheltered viewpoint might place before you an expansive panorama of sea and islands stretching several kilometres from where you stand. It is truly a diverse region and it is from that diversity that the uniqueness of the Gulf Islands is derived.

With the exception of Saltspring's mountainous south end, the Gulf Islands are low in elevation by comparison with British Columbia's lower mainland and Vancouver Island. While some peaks, such as Mount Galiano, Mount Parke on Mayne, or George Hill on North Pender, are prominent landmarks when seen from the deck of a ferry, it is more often the uninhabited islets, the long, pastoral valleys or unusual sandstone formations which linger long in the memories of island visitors.

Coon Bay on Galiano.

Though the Gulf Islands are considered low-lying by southern B.C. standards, they nonetheless have a mountainous appearance. Much of the shoreline is rugged, with steep, sheer cliffs plunging to the sea. Most of the valleys are narrow, dominated by tree-covered ridges which slope to sea-level fields and farms. So gradual are some of these inland slopes that the climb is hardly noticeable to someone driving a valley road in a car. The road from Fulford Harbour to Ganges on Saltspring, for instance, climbs and descends several hills as it winds out of the Fulford Valley, but the overall climb occurs over such a distance that few drivers realize they have reached a height of about 120 metres by the time they pass Cusheon Lake Road.

The Gulf Islands consist primarily of sedimentary rock such as sandstone, conglomerate, shale and siltstone. The sandstone is particularly noticeable in areas like East Point on Saturna or Cain Peninsula on Galiano, where the persistent pounding of the sea through untold millenniums has carved deep pockets and weird formations. The sandstone has a sandpapery texture and in some areas looks much like huge slabs of smooth, flat rock which have been placed on top of one another and melted together at the seams. In areas of abundant sandstone there are usually significant deposits of conglomerate, a harder rock which looks like millions of pebbles cemented together and dumped on the beach. The southern half of Saltspring, where the bedrock is comprised mainly of metamorphic or volcanic rock, is more like Vancouver Island than most of the other Gulf Islands.

Mineral potential on the Gulf Islands is considered low but deposits of rhodonite, iron, shale and even gold have been found on Saltspring, and gravel is dug from pits on some islands. B.C. Lightweight Aggregates operated a shale-expanding plant on Saturna Island between 1959 and 1975.

The topography and type of bedrock have a major influence on the vegetation. The dominant tree species throughout the islands is Douglas fir, some as high as 75 metres and measuring nearly two metres in diameter. Most Douglas firs on the islands are in the 30- to 40-metre range with diameters of about a metre or less. Grand fir and western red cedar grow on well-drained, gradual slopes while Garry oak and arbutus thrive in shallow soils where drainage is rapid and the land is dry.

Garry oak and arbutus are found in Canada only on the west coast. Arbutus trees, known as Pacific madrones in the United States, are Canada's only broad-leafed evergreens and, unlike deciduous trees, they keep their leaves through winter and produce a bright red berry, strikingly similar to those which grow on holly trees at Christmas time. Some grow to 30 metres in height with trunks up to a metre in diameter.

Garry oaks, with dark gray bark and twisted limbs, are found only along the west coast of North America from California to Vancouver Island

and occur up the east coast of Vancouver Island as far as Courtenay. They are plentiful in the Gulf Islands but grow only in a few isolated groves on the mainland. These majestic giants are Canada's only native oak tree on the west coast. Although oak wood is valuable as a decorative material, there is no significant commercial production of Garry oak in British Columbia.

The underbrush in the Gulf Islands forests is mainly plants such as salal, salmonberry and red huckleberry, with bracken and sword fern in damper areas. The islands' mild climate is particularly conducive to wildflower growth, and a wide variety of colourful spring flowers blooms every year throughout the islands. Stonecrop, blue camas, satin flower, shooting star and white fawn lily are among the species which embellish the sunny hillsides of the Gulf Islands each spring. Most of these flowers grow in the same open areas as Garry oak and arbutus trees, where the land is dry and soil is shallow.

Garry oak on Saltspring.

Gulf Islands Wildlife

Wildlife in the Gulf Islands is as varied as it is abundant. Blacktail deer roam the islands and while many islanders appreciate the sight of them, others, like vegetable gardeners, consider them a menace. Raccoons, mink and river otters are often seen on Gulf Island beaches, and seals and sea lions are frequently observed offshore.

There are more than 200 bird species in the Gulf Islands and half of them nest here. Besides peregrine falcons, hawks, owls, eagles and other raptors, interesting birds include kingfishers, woodpeckers, pheasants, grouse, ravens, California quail and turkey vultures.

The waters around the islands are home for a multitude of marine animals. On the surface you may see seals, sea lions, whales, porpoises and dolphins. Beneath the surface there are five salmon species, perch, herring, dogfish, halibut and a variety of bottomfish. There are numerous shellfish such as crabs, oysters, clams, mussels, scallops, abalone, urchins, barnacles, shrimp and prawns, as well as some 90 species of sea stars.

Sea Lions — A Tonne of Blubber and Fur

Both Steller's and California sea lions roam the Gulf Islands and are frequently spotted by beachcombers and boaters. B.C. has a stable breeding population of about 6,000 Steller's sea lions. More than 1,000 may winter in southern B.C., about 400 of them in the southern Gulf Islands. As many as 3,000 California sea lions move up the coast to winter in southern B.C.

The auburn-coloured northern, or Steller's, sea lion is native to B.C. A full-grown Steller's bull is a tonne of blubber and fur, twice the size of the largest grizzly bear, yet it moves with a speed and agility that belies its bulky form. Out of water the sea lion appears sluggish, propped up awkwardly on its fore-flippers, mindful of its vulnerability to terrestrial creatures like man. But in the sea it swims gracefully throughout its domain, fearing only the killer whale.

Sea lions in southern B.C. are mainly a wintering mammal, arriving from their northern breeding rookeries in September and staying until April or May. Some winters as many as 400 haul out on the Belle Chain Islets, near Saturna Island. Sharp-sighted ferry passengers often see them swimming near Collinson Reef and Helen Point, at the southwest entrance to Active Pass. Occasional sightings come from Porlier Pass, East Point, Plumper Sound and the south end of Saltspring Island.

Though sea lions in Canada are protected by law they have become the focus of a coastal controversy because some people believe their populations are out of control. Sea lions are predators which innocently hunt a prey valuable to man — herring and salmon. Some fishermen believe sea lions affect their livelihoods, and as more sea lions appear along the B.C. coast, both sport and commercial fishermen renew their call for population controls. It's a case of history repeating itself.

A decade past the turn of the century, fishermen complained that flourishing herds of Steller's sea lions were devouring a healthy share of the annual salmon and herring harvests. Sea lions were of no value, they argued, so the federal government quelled their complaints in 1913 with the first study of B.C. sea lions. The study concluded the fishermen were right: the only good sea lion was a dead sea lion, so a bounty was offered on their snouts.

The bounty, however, did little to reduce the numbers of sea lions, so the federal government ordered its fisheries officers to slaughter them on the breeding rookeries. They shot them in their mating territories and surrounding rocks. They shot them at feeding grounds, at haul-outs and resting waters. In the late 1960s, environmentalists rallied against the "control program" and convinced Parliament, in 1970, to protect all marine mammals under the Fisheries Act.

Today, B.C.'s 6,000-odd breeding Steller's are about one-third of the traditional breeding numbers. They return to a few breeding rookeries in northern waters where more than 1,000 pups are born each season, just enough to replace those which die, leaving a stable population. Unburdened by newborn offspring, the males disperse from the breeding rocks and many travel down the coast to the Gulf Islands. The females remain within a few kilometres of the breeding grounds throughout the year.

Wild sea lions are generally not aggressive or timid but they could

Sea lions.

be unpredictable if spooked. They usually can be approached to within a few metres and noise from outboard motors doesn't appear to bother them.

Harbour Seals — Cautious but Curious

Harbour seals, smaller cousins of the sea lion, are plentiful around the islands and are commonly seen basking lazily in the sun, cigar-shaped bodies high and dry at low tide. Boaters and beachcombers often see their bald heads and whiskery snouts slinking quietly along the surface of the sea.

While wildlife lovers enjoy watching harbour seals, some sport fishermen wish they weren't so plentiful. They're clever creatures, and a growing number of seals are learning to find easy meals by hanging around popular sport fishing waters. When they hear the sound of line zinging from a fisherman's reel, they simply swim up behind the hooked fish and grab it.

They breed in local waters and since 1970, when seals became protected by law, their numbers in B.C. have grown from about 10,000 to about 75,000 and are continuing to grow by 10 or 12 per cent a year. There are probably well over 13,000 in Georgia Strait. It's estimated that bounties in Canada claimed an average of 3,000 seals a year between 1928 and 1964, and an equal number of seals were likely killed by people who didn't claim bounties. A commercial hunt in the late 1960s also eliminated about 10,000 harbour seals.

Seals in the Gulf Islands are cautious but curious, and will often venture close to a drifting boat.

Whales and Porpoises

An exciting but infrequent sight in Gulf Island waters is the tall, black dorsal fin of a killer whale breaking the surface as it rises for a breath of air. More often than not, these misnamed mammals travel in pods, or families, and three or four may surface simultaneously. Only about 300 inhabit B.C. waters.

A killer whale breaking the surface and shooting spurts of mist from its blowhole, only a few metres from where you sit, is undoubtedly one of the most startling, awesome sights to be seen anywhere. It is difficult for terrestrial beings like ourselves to imagine these magnificent beasts roaming the sea around us, travelling in closely-knit families, communicating among themselves over great distances. Once you have seen them at close range, close enough to hear that unmistakable rush of air firing from the lungs, you will always watch for them again.

Once considered a nuisance by fishermen and mariners, the killer whale, also known as orca, has only recently aroused the curiosity of scientists, and earned long-overdue respect for its apparent intelligence and mysterious communicative abilities. They are toothed whales, bulls measuring more than nine metres long, and cows about six. The tall dorsal fin of a male can be as high as two metres. They are primarily black, with patches of white on their undersides and lower back.

In the Gulf Islands these whales are seen outside the entrances to Active Pass, occasionally in the pass, off East Point on Saturna Island, and along some of the shorelines bordering Georgia Strait. There are times when they enter inside waters and a few are inevitably seen by fishermen and boaters. Visitors to Musgrave Landing, on Saltspring Island, may hear the exploding sound of the whales exhaling as they travel down Sansum Narrows toward Saanich Inlet. The sound is remarkably like gunshots followed by a short echo.

Gray whales and humpbacks, much larger than killer whales, occasionally enter Gulf Island waters but not as often as killer whales. Risso's Dolphins, about half the size of killer whales, are dark gray, almost black, and are sometimes seen around Gulf Island waters. More common in the islands are Harbour and Dall's porpoises, both about two metres long. They are the smallest of the toothed whales and travel in small groups. Boaters and ferry passengers may mistake them for killer whales.

Seabirds and Herons

The Gulf Islands lie on the western edge of the Pacific flyway, and more than a million migratory birds grace the spring and autumn skies

Cormorants on Mandarte Island.

11

over the islands. The distant honking of Canada geese may prompt you to look overhead and see dozens, if not hundreds, of these beautiful birds flying in an orderly, V-shaped formation.

Not all Gulf Island birds are just passing through. Over 4,000 pairs of double-crested and pelagic cormorants, glaucous-winged gulls, pigeon guillemots and tufted puffins nest in more than two dozen colonies in the Gulf Islands and on the eastern edge of southern Vancouver Island.

Always an eye-catcher is the great blue heron, whose throaty croak is a startling sound to an unsuspecting bird watcher. These spindle-legged, stork-like birds spend their days wading the shallows in search of seashore delicacies, standing motionless until an unwary victim swims within striking distance. They nest in treetop colonies, known as heronries, where they build enormous nests of sticks and twigs. The largest Gulf Island heronry is located on Sidney Island. Another nesting colony is near Crofton, across Stuart Channel from Saltspring Island.

Loons — Crazy, They Say

If you're camped on the shore of a Gulf Island you may be haunted through the night by the ghostly laughter of a loon. It echoes across the water, piercing the darkness as you lie awake in your tent: though you want to sleep, you can't help listening for it again. It's the call of a maniac — crazy as a loon, they say — and in spite of its persistence it startles you each time you hear it.

As you wait in the pre-dawn glow for sunrise, think of the Alaskan Indian tale about the loon. Long, long ago, the legend says, a group of Tlingit people in canoes were lost in the dark. They heard the melancholy wail of a loon and followed the cry until the bird appeared. It swam ahead of their canoes, leading them into daylight.

As the sun rises you may see the checkered back of the loon. The common loon, clad in striking summer plumage, with a velvet black head and string of pearls around its neck, looks as though someone tossed seashells, bleached by the sun, onto its back. According to the folklore of northern B.C.'s Dene Indians, that's precisely what happened.

In the story of how the loon got its necklace, there was a blind man whose wife helped him hunt. But after many years she became tired of looking after a blind man and left him. The old man sat by a lake, crying loudly and sadly, until a loon came and asked why he cried.

"Alas," replied the man, "I am blind and my wife has left me."

"Come to me and sit on my back and bury your eyes in the down of my neck," said the loon.

Together they plunged beneath the water and when they came to the surface the loon asked: "Can you see now?"

"I see a little, as though through a mist," the man replied.

The loon dived again and when they surfaced the old man could see clearly. In appreciation he gave the loon his most prized possession, a necklace of white shells. He tossed it toward the bird and it settled around its neck. Then he took other shells from his quiver and threw them toward the loon. They settled on its back and have remained there since.

The common loon is one of five species to inhabit the coastal waters of B.C. It's a big diving bird, sometimes nearly a metre long, and it lies low in the water as it patrols in search of fish. Its name may be misleading in B.C. because it's not the most common loon here. Its smaller cousin, the Pacific loon, is often seen in huge flocks migrating in spring through Juan de Fuca and Georgia straits to its northern nesting grounds.

The Pacific loon is the most gregarious of the loons, gathering by the thousands in areas where tidal upwellings stir up feasts of herring, minnows, or anchovies. One of these places is Active Pass, between Galiano and Mayne islands: on certain days in April passengers aboard B.C. ferries may see as many as 10,000 Pacific loons fishing and resting.

Propelled by powerful, paddle-like feet, the loon dives to great depths to catch fish. There are records of loons being caught in fishnets 60 metres below the surface. They dive forward in a quick roll, exposing the tips of their stubby wings for a split second before disappearing. Sometimes a loon will expel the air from its lungs and simply sink from sight, leaving no trace of having been there. In their muscles, loons have large amounts of myoglobin, a respiratory pigment that allows them to store oxygen for use underwater.

By early or mid-May most of these migrating Pacific loons have left Active Pass and the Gulf Islands and are heading toward their breeding grounds in northern B.C. and beyond. The enormous flocks which move up the coast are impressive: during the latter half of May more than 150,000 loons are known to fly past Brooks Peninsula, on the northwest coast of Vancouver Island. Although the loon has difficulty taking off, running upwind along the surface of the water, it's a powerful flier once it's airborne, covering vast distances at speeds up to 100 kilometres an hour.

As they reach the north the flocks split up and the birds settle on forested lakes or ponds, generally between Atlin and the Liard River. They're solitary nesters, returning each year to breed in the same areas. The loon rarely leaves the water except to fly and breed, and it's during the nesting season that the unfortunate loon's ponderousness becomes difficult to conceal. The loon was designed to swim, with legs set so far back that when it hauls itself from the water it often flops forward on its breast when it tries to move too quickly. The word loon comes from a Scandinavian word, *lom*, meaning lame or clumsy person. It's rather unfair when you consider the loon's enviable efficiency in water.

The northern nesting grounds are usually in isolated, uninhabited places, and it's here that the loon has earned its reputation as a symbol of true wilderness. Hundreds of loons winter in the Gulf Islands, and although the loon may winter as far south as California, it is inevitably associated with the loneliness and tranquility of the north. It is a restless bird and in some parts of the world it's believed the loon is particularly vocal before bouts of bad weather.

The loon never seems to sleep: its long, laughing music, as distinctive as the howl of a wolf, carries on through the night. For some people it's a crazy, unsettling cry: for others it's a soothing companion in an otherwise lonesome place. But regardless of how the cry of the loon arouses the imagination, few who have heard it would deny it's the true call of the wild.

Bald Eagles — From Bounties to Bountiful

A bald eagle soaring along the face of a cliff, or boldly perched at the top of a Douglas fir, is a sight that grabs even the most moderate bird watcher. There's a certain nobility to birds of prey: to see one hunting is a rare privilege. From the top of a tree the eagle selects its prey, possibly a coot or a duck from a flock floating on a bay or lagoon. One ill-fated straggler is singled out and the great white-headed predator lunges, forcing its prey to dive. The bird surfaces and the eagle strikes, scarcely allowing time for a breath of air. The bird dives, surfaces, and the eagle persists, again and again until its quarry is too exhausted to seek refuge in the depths of the bay. The attack is over in moments. The eagle unceremoniously snatches its enfeebled victim from the water and leaves as quickly, as quietly, as it came.

The bald eagle's unparalleled hunting skills are a paradox, the cause of both its salvation and its demise. Possibly the most versatile predator in Canada and probably the most resourceful bird of prey on the continent, the bald eagle, like the golden eagle which inhabits B.C. in small numbers, was among the most persecuted raptors in North America until the early 1960s, when new laws declared it a protected species. Although the bald eagle is the emblem of the United States, Americans and Canadians alike considered this heraldic bird vermin, a sheep and poultry killer for which a government-sponsored bounty was offered as a means of exterminating it. It is believed today that the number of bald eagles which survive outside B.C. and Alaska is smaller than the total number killed in Alaska in the days when the carnage was encouraged.

Despite the senseless extermination efforts of former generations, bald eagles remain plentiful on the north Pacific coast. It is estimated today that as many as 16,000 adult eagles inhabit B.C., particularly along the jagged, forested coast, and substantially more thrive on the coastal waterways of Alaska. There is no indication that their numbers are dwindling and in some areas their populations appear to be growing. This stately predator, one of 34 raptorial bird species in B.C., has an immense range, spreading from Labrador across the continent and south to Florida and Mexico, but their numbers are limited outside the North Pacific. Nearly all of the bald eagles in the world live in British Columbia and Alaska.

The bald eagle is associated almost exclusively with large bodies of water, and though some inhabit inland lakes and rivers, it is primarily a

Bald eagle.

maritime bird, relying on the prolific seabird and marine life of the coast as its major food source. Autumn and early winter salmon runs are particularly attractive to eagles, and hundreds congregate along B.C. rivers to feed on fish carcasses, a habit which has unjustly earned these birds a reputation as scavengers.

Eagles are seafood gourmets, proficient fishermen and hunters that stalk rocky shorelines and beaches, probing seaweed and poking in tidal pools for shellfish and crabs. Biologists who climbed into an eagle nest in the Queen Charlotte Islands were surprised to find 357 abalone shells. It is not uncommon to see an eagle swoop from a shore-side branch and clench an unwary fish swimming near the surface. If small fish such as herring are plentiful, an eagle can devour one in mid-flight before diving in for another catch. Larger fish, up to three kilograms, which unwisely swim near the surface are also fair game. The eagle circles overhead until a fish is sighted, then descends and sinks its talons into the flesh. Unable to return to flight, the eagle uses its wings to swim with the fish in tow. Occasionally eagles drown trying to make it to shore.

While the eagle's reputation as a scavenger may be unjust, it is well known as a pirate. In many cases the loser is a hard-working osprey, an equally proficient fisherman but a reluctant defender of its catch against a determined eagle. The eagle, with its 2.2-metre wingspan, chases the osprey in flight, forcing it to drop its catch for the eagle to retrieve. It is with similar deftness that the eagle preys upon loons, seagulls, coots, ducks and storm petrels.

The eagle's nesting habits are as intriguing as its hunting methods. Partners for life, each pair returns to the same nest year after year, to lay the eggs and share incubation duties. Only fully mature five-year-olds, with distinctive white heads and tails, pair up to breed. A mature bird may measure almost a metre from its tail to its head and weigh between 2.5 and 6.3 kilograms, the female being one-third larger than its mate.

Huge stick nests, which when first built usually measure about a metre across by 60 centimetres deep, are constructed within the crown of mature conifers. Occasionally nests are made on cliffs and there have been instances where nests were discovered on the ground in coastal forests. The inside of the nests are lined with soft materials, such as seaweed or grasses, and each year about 20 kilograms of material are added. Nests weighing a tonne are common. One nest found in an old cedar tree on Bonilla Island, on the north coast of B.C., measured 6.6 metres across and 4.8 metres deep. It was impossible to estimate its weight but researchers believed it was at least half a century old. It eventually toppled out of the tree, as many nests do.

It was once thought that bald eagles travelled only short distances throughout the year but studies now have shown they are migratory. Migrations begin after the young have fledged, by September or October.

The distances some eagles travel are astounding when one considers they were believed to be a non-migratory bird. Two eagles banded in the Chilkat River area of Alaska during late fall were found on Vancouver Island in late winter. In another survey, eagles wearing radio transmitters and banded in Washington's Skagit Valley were later located on the Queen Charlotte Islands.

Eagle watching is an intriguing year-round pastime in the Gulf Islands. Eagles are common throughout the islands and in early spring as many as 70 at a time may be seen in the trees on Mayne Island along the shores of Active Pass. After March, when nesting begins, the simplest way to locate eagles is to travel about 200 metres offshore in a boat. Using binoculars, look for "eagle trees," tall snags that are favourite perches for bald eagles. If you spot an individual eagle, scan the tallest nearby trees, from about halfway up to the top, for the nest or the mate.

Gulf Islands Weather — Canada's Finest

The Gulf Islands lie comfortably in the rain shadow of the Vancouver Island mountains, sheltered from the ruthless rains so well known to inhabitants of Vancouver Island's west coast. The differences in weather between the east and west sides of Vancouver Island are profound when one considers that the distance between the two is less than 120 kilometres at the southern end. Yet while Gulf Islanders, on the east side of Vancouver Island, enjoy a Mediterranean-type climate with dry, cool summers, mild, damp winters and annual precipitation of about 84 centimetres, people on the west coast endure an average of more than 250 centimetres of rain a year.

The Gulf Island area also enjoys the longest frost-free season in Canada, more than eight months. Gonzales Observatory in Victoria is the only official weather station in Canada which has actually experienced an entire winter when the thermometer did not drop below freezing.

The following statistics are provided by the Victoria Weather Office of Environment Canada. They are based on many years of readings from climate stations in the Gulf Islands and on southeastern Vancouver Island.

Sunshine

Hours of bright sunshine, based on readings from stations at Cowichan Bay, Nanaimo, Saanichton and Victoria:

January	February	March	April	May	June	
59	88	135	190	251	249	

July	August	September	October	November	December	Year
313	278	196	122	68	54	2003

Precipitation

Mean total precipitation in centimetres, based on readings from two climate stations on Saltspring Island and one on Pender:

January	February	March	April	May	June
14.3	9.3	7.6	4.7	3.2	3.2

July	August	September	October	November	December	Year
1.9	2.5	3.6	9	10	14.6	83.9

Temperature

Mean daily temperatures in Celsius, including mean daily maximum and minimum temperatures, based on readings from two stations on Saltspring:

	Jan	Feb	Mar	Apr	May	Jun	Jul	Aug	Sept	Oct	Nov	Dec	Year
Mean:	3	5	6	9	12	15	17	17	15	11	6	4	10
Maximum:	6	8	10	14	17	20	23	22	19	14	9	7	14
Minimum:	0	2	2	4	7	10	12	12	9	7	3	2	6

The People of the Islands

In 1857 Saltspring became the first Gulf Island to be settled. Farming was the chief occupation of the pioneers and by the turn of the century there were 80 farms on Saltspring Island. People spread to other islands where farming was also the primary industry, but transporting commodities to Vancouver Island and mainland markets was a drawback which always plagued Gulf Island farmers. The fishing industry played a significant role in the lives of early settlers, with salteries and fish reduction plants scattered throughout the islands. Whaling, logging and sawmilling were also among industries developed by island pioneers.

Tourist resorts were commonplace in the Gulf Islands as early as 1900, and tourism today is a major factor in the islands' economy. A boom in subdivisions for vacation and retirement homes occurred in the 1960s, after improved ferry service made the tranquil, rural atmosphere of the Gulf Islands accessible to people from high-population areas such as the B.C. lower mainland and southern Vancouver Island.

Many of the industries developed in the late 1800s and early 1900s have lost their significance in the overall economy, but few have completely disappeared. Logging, log booming, small-scale sawmilling and shake splitting have survived, a small, island-based fishing fleet still exists, and although farming is not overly profitable there is a move to revive the industry.

With substantial population increases, service industries involving schools, highways, ferries, hospitals and government have grown. Ganges, Saltspring's unincorporated village, is the largest community in the Gulf Islands and the main retail centre for Saltspring.

The permanent population of Saltspring and the outer islands has more than doubled since the late 1960s and there is no indication that the growth will slow down, despite rising land costs and shortages of water. More than one-third of the Gulf Islands' permanent residents are older than 55 and the population older than 65 is the highest, on a per-capita basis, in British Columbia. Many of these islanders are retired people who have left a cross-section of city jobs, bringing with them an incredible variety of opinions, attitudes and educational and occupational backgrounds.

The people of the Gulf Islands are independent by necessity and evidence of their independence is shown in the recent turn to home occupations such as boatbuilding, instrument making, carving, weaving, pottery and crafts production. There has been a steady influx of writers, painters, sculptors and other artists in recent years; many of them are able to enjoy an individualistic lifestyle, while earning a modest living.

Few people move from cities to the Gulf Islands without being prepared to earn a living doing an assortment of odd jobs or practising an occupation which is likely to produce only a moderate income. Average family incomes, as a result, are slightly lower on the Gulf Islands than in other rural communities in B.C. While a few Saltspring and Pender islanders commute daily to Vancouver Island for work, most permanent residents are able to get by with on-island employment.

Some Gulf Islanders don't leave their island for years at a time: they're comfortable with an independent existence in a place where you set your own standards and move at your own pace.

Islands Trust — Gulf Islands Government

The beauty and uniqueness of the Gulf Islands have been known to the people of the Pacific Northwest for generations, but it was not until the early 1970s that the British Columbia government recognized the need to protect these unusual islands from unwarranted development. An all-party committee of the provincial legislature was asked to determine the special needs of these islands and the result of the committee's recommendations was the formation, in 1974, of the Islands Trust, a group of 26 elected islanders empowered to "protect and preserve" the islands in the Gulf of Georgia. The power of the Islands Trust was strengthened with the enactment of a new Islands Trust Act in 1990.

Under the legislation, two representatives from each of 13 designated islands are elected for three-year terms as local trustees who together form

19

the Trust Council. These local trustees elect, from among their ranks, a chair and two vice-chairs to serve as the executive. Land use on each designated island is managed separately by a group composed of two local trustees and a member of the executive.

There are, of course, many more than 13 islands in the Gulf of Georgia so, under the act, another 177 lesser islands are attached to the 13 designated islands to be governed by the trustees. Sidney Island, for example, is one of the lesser islands and falls under jurisdiction of North Pender. It is therefore managed by the trustees and executive member responsible for North Pender.

The executive committee is also responsible for some 50 other islands which are not among the 13 designated or 177 lesser islands.

The Islands Trust has the power to regulate property development through zoning bylaws. Although some developers think of the Islands Trust as a nuisance, many islanders are grateful that the future of the Gulf Islands is under the control of people who live on them.

Under the new Islands Trust Act, the Islands Trust is empowered to hold land. Special sites and features in the islands now can be preserved, through the Islands Trust, for future generations. A joint study by the Islands Trust and the Nature Conservancy of Canada produced an inventory of natural areas in the Gulf Islands and made recommendations concerning conservation of these areas. Under one section of the report, entitled "Need for Preservation in the Islands Trust Area," the report has this to say: "The Islands Trust Area, as part of the Strait of Georgia-Puget Sound region, can readily be considered the most important area for outdoor recreation in North America. Few other areas of the world offer such a diversity of recreational and aesthetic values. In addition, the area's dry, mild climate, outstanding marine resources and unique flora and fauna make it one of the most interesting environmental regions in Canada."

Gulf Islands Real Estate — Favoured by British Columbians

There has been a proliferation in both permanent and seasonal populations on the Gulf Islands in recent years, caused partly by better transportation to the islands. There has been a general misconception among some islanders and non-islanders alike that a substantial amount of Gulf Island property is owned by Americans. However, a survey of the islands, conducted shortly before this book was written, shows that only 5 per cent of the lots are owned by Americans, mainly from Washington and California.

The same survey shows that nearly 83 per cent of the lots are owned by British Columbians. More than 65 per cent of the B.C. owners are from

Vancouver, nearly 13 per cent from Victoria, more than 13 per cent from the same island and another 9 per cent from other parts of the province. About 11 per cent of the lots are owned by Canadians from outside B.C., primarily Alberta, and slightly more than .5 of 1 per cent are owned by people from overseas countries.

Lot prices on the Gulf Islands are influenced by the same factors that affect properties in other parts of B.C., but scarcity on the islands is an added contributor to rising prices. Property values on the islands have skyrocketed in the recent past.

Land prices on the Gulf Islands will inevitably continue to climb with the demand, although prices could also be affected by shortages of domestic water. Increasing property values, however, are already having an adverse effect on owners unable to afford the taxes. Particularly hurt are non-resident owners who purchased recreational or seasonal homes when prices were low. The values have since been boosted by favourable market conditions and these owners have been hit by sizeable, often unaffordable tax increases. Families who own land passed down through generations are facing similar tax difficulties even though there are no mortgage debts against their lands.

There are real estate firms operating throughout the islands to help people interested in Gulf Island property and the *Gulf Islands Driftwood* publishes a number of pages of real estate advertisements every week.

No Trespassing — The Property Owner's Privilege

There is a disturbing lack of public places on the Gulf Islands, and although there are some local and provincial parks, their numbers are

Saturna Island cottage.

21

inadequate to accommodate the growing number of visitors. Some owners of large properties allow people to hike or camp on their land if the visitors are considerate enough to ask permission first. Other property owners, however, will not tolerate trespassers under any circumstances and there have been incidents when outsiders have been asked, quite unlawfully, to leave public areas.

Many of the public areas, such as parks and recreational reserves, are specifically noted in this book. Most beaches in British Columbia are public property up to the highest high tide line, which is where the driftwood ends. There are places where waterfront owners have been granted foreshore rights, giving them the privilege of using the beach for some personal purpose such as wharf or boat ramp construction.

Tides in summer are generally lower than in winter and it is possible to camp or picnic on a beach without worrying about the tide washing away your tent, or trespassing on private land. Camping is prohibited or discouraged on some beaches due to fire hazards, and many beaches are inaccessible, except by boat, because they are surrounded by private property with no public access between lots.

The rights of Gulf Island property owners deserve the utmost respect, but so do the rights of the public. In short, stay off private property if you do not have permission to use it, but remember, the beaches belong to everyone.

Fire — A Serious Threat to the Islands

In the summer of 1976 some mindless imbecile flicked a cigarette butt from the top of Saltspring's Mount Maxwell and started a fire which destroyed more than two hectares of forestland and took nearly a week to extinguish and clean up. It started at the base of the mountain, where access is poor and water is not available. Water had to be backpacked up the mountain to the fire and five days of concentrated effort finally ended the ordeal.

Fire is the *number one threat* to the Gulf Islands and careless smoking is the number one cause of accidental fires. More than 60 per cent of all accidental fires on the islands are started by thoughtless or ignorant smokers who illustrate an appalling disrespect for these beautiful islands each time they toss a lighted cigarette out the window of a moving car or chuck a burning butt off to the side of a hiking trail.

The Gulf Islands are particularly susceptible to fires because of the low rainfall and droughts in the warmer months, mainly summer. Access to much of the rugged terrain is extremely difficult, especially with firefighting equipment, and many of the high, rough, rock faces are covered during summer with tinder-dry mosses, lichen and grasses — vegetation referred to as "flash fuels" by the British Columbia Forest Service.

Like many rural areas, the Gulf Islands are protected from fire primarily by volunteer firefighters, who must depend upon the common sense of the public to minimize fire hazards on the islands. Some islands, such as Saltspring and Mayne, have their own bylaws regulating fires and permits to light them, while other islands issue permits under regulations of the provincial Forest Act. Burning permits for open fires are issued through local fire departments or by people authorized by the B.C. Forest Service to distribute them. Check with locals or at island stores to find out how a permit can be acquired.

Under normal conditions, campfires are allowed without permits on crown land, such as beaches below the high tide mark. There are, however, some regulations which must be obeyed when lighting campfires. A campfire must not be ignited within three metres of stumps, logs, overhanging trees, or buildings, or within 15 metres of flammable debris such as slash or dry grass. Debris like grass or moss must be cleared within one metre of the fire and the fire itself must not be more than a metre wide and a metre high. A shovel or pail of water must always be kept near the fire and the fire must be extinguished so the coals are cold enough to pick up with your bare hand.

It is important to note, however, that fires are banned in some areas, which are usually signposted. Also, the B.C. Forest Service prohibits all fires during periods of extreme drought, generally every August. These prohibitions are heavily advertised on radio and television and in newspapers, and are strictly enforced. Fines and jail terms can be ordered for people convicted of violating fire regulations. People who cause a fire through carelessness or violation of law can also be ordered to pay costs of damage and fighting the fire, a figure which could be in the hundreds of thousands of dollars.

The B.C. Forest Service has a toll-free telephone number to call and report forest fires. Anyone who spots what appears to be a forest fire is asked to call Zenith-5555.

Marine Transportation — It Wasn't Always So Simple

It may seem far-fetched to link the Fraser River gold rush of 1858 with ferry service in the Gulf Islands, but it could be said that the frantic search for the mother lode on the British Columbia mainland laid the foundation for steamship service between Vancouver Island and the mainland. When the cry of "gold" drifted down the coast as far as California, Fort Victoria was inundated by treasure seekers. Eight hundred transients

23

spent the winter of 1858 at Fort Victoria, and by spring of that year more than 22,000 gold miners were camped outside the fort.

The gold rush attracted thousands from Vancouver Island, many who rowed from Victoria, up the eastern side of Saanich Peninsula, through Active Pass and across Georgia Strait to the mainland. Miners Bay, midway through Active Pass on Mayne Island, is named for the fortune-hunters who stopped overnight before heading into the often inhospitable waters of the strait.

Otter Bay on North Pender.

It soon became clear that permanent service to the mainland would be profitable and the route through the Gulf Islands was practical. Active Pass, in fact, is named after a wooden paddlesteamer which was originally christened *Gold Hunter*. The ship was used to carry gold seekers between the Isthmus of Panama and San Francisco until it was purchased by the United States government, renamed *Active* and used to help survey the 49th parallel in Georgia Strait. She was the first ship to navigate Active Pass, a channel which has become the busiest waterway in the Gulf Islands.

Georgia Strait was originally named the Gulf of Georgia by Captain George Vancouver, of the Royal Navy, in 1792, in honour of King George III. It was not until 73 years later, in 1865, that Admiral Sir George Henry Richards altered the name to Georgia Strait, but even today it is locally referred to as the "Gulf of Georgia" or simply the "Gulf."

Many of the province's coastal waterways were dominated after the turn of the century by ships of the Canadian Pacific Railway, built as small ocean liners with luxurious dining saloons and staterooms. Other steamships provided transportation to and from the islands as well as from island to island.

One of the best-remembered Gulf Island ships was the ill-fated *S.S. Iroquois*, a 198-tonne steamer, measuring 25 metres and drawing slightly more than two metres of water. Built in 1900, the little ship served the Gulf Islands until she met an untimely death on April 10, 1911. Seas were high when the *Iroquois* pulled away from the wharf in Sidney, laden with 10 tonnes of phosphate fertilizer in the bow and feed, bar iron and general merchandise, including 30 tonnes of hay, piled high on the decks. Friends and relatives of the passengers watched in horror as the heavy cargo shifted. The *Iroquois* foundered less than two kilometres from the wharf and sank in 30 metres of water, killing the 21 people aboard. Her deteriorating hulk was discovered by scuba divers in 1977 and many of the artifacts have since been retrieved.

Various other privately owned vessels such as the *Cy Peck* and the *Lady Rose* served the Gulf Islands. It wasn't until Vancouver Island was cut off from the mainland in 1958 by a seamen's strike that the provincial government started thinking about going into the public ferry business.

Victoria's politicians first came up with a partnership scheme involving private ferry companies and the government, but nobody was interested. So, in 1959, the government announced its intentions to operate its own ferries, and the following year the *Queen of Sidney* and *Queen of Tsawwassen* were built. An existing Gulf Island service was purchased in 1961 and expanded. B.C. Ferries, now a crown corporation, today operates more than three dozen ships on two dozen routes.

The two original B.C. ferries, still in service, are 100 metres long overall and have carrying capacities of more than 130 cars and nearly 1,000 passengers. They travel at about 18 knots.

25

The *Queen of Nanaimo*, a ship often used on Gulf Island runs, was built in Victoria in 1964. A total of 130 metres long, she carries 190 cars and nearly 1,200 passengers.

Other ferries you may see on Gulf Island runs include the *Bowen Queen*, built in Victoria in 1965. She was stretched in 1979 from 63 metres long to 85 metres, increasing the vehicle capacity from 50 to 70. Her sister ship, the *Mayne Queen*, also was stretched in 1979. The *Saltspring Queen* is a 44-metre vessel built in 1949. With a capacity of 130 passengers and 36 cars, she travels at 9 knots. The *Quinitsa*, built in Vancouver in 1977, is 75 metres long, carries 50 cars and 349 passengers, and runs at 12 knots. One of the smallest ships in the fleet, the *Nicola*, is 34 metres long. Built in Vancouver in 1960, she carries only 16 vehicles and 129 passengers at a cruising speed of 10 knots.

Travellers from both sides of Georgia Strait can take ferries directly to the Gulf Islands. Ships depart regularly from Tsawwassen on the mainland. Reservations are highly recommended and, in fact, are required at busy times for vehicles, but not for passengers. Check telephone directories for B.C. Ferry numbers.

Ferries also depart regularly from Swartz Bay to Saltspring and the outer islands. Reservations are not available for travel from Swartz Bay, or for inter-island travel.

Ferry traffic is often heavy during summer, and on holiday weekends throughout the year. There can be waits at terminals. Travel time aboard varies with routes and the number of stops before your destination. A ferry travelling inter-island before going on to the mainland, for example, could make as many as three stops before reaching its final destination. If you're travelling with children, it's wise to pack lots of activities to keep them busy.

Information

Tourist information on the Gulf Islands is available from several sources. In B.C. there are nine tourism regions, each with its own association. Many businesses on the Gulf Islands belong to the Tourism Association of Vancouver Island and information concerning those businesses is available from the association, which is listed in telephone directories.

There is also a Travel Infocentre Network, which works with the provincial government to promote travel in B.C. Travel Infocentres in most communities are operated by chambers of commerce, providing information about their own regions as well as other parts of the province. Operation of these infocentres on the Gulf Islands may vary from year to year — sometimes they're there, sometimes they're not, depending on the situation of the local business community. Those in operation may be open year-round or seasonally, again depending on local businesses. Most are located in conspicuous places, such as ferry terminals, business centres or main highways.

Chambers of commerce on the islands may be listed in telephone directories. Like Travel Infocentres, however, chambers of commerce in small communities come and go. Whether or not a chamber exists, Gulf Island businesses are normally helpful to tourists: you can find a business or resort in a telephone directory and call it.

The *Gulf Islands Driftwood*, established in 1960, is an excellent weekly newspaper covering the events and issues of the Gulf Islands. Published at Ganges, on Saltspring, the paper is good reading for anyone with an interest in island news, and gossip. Both the news and advertisements are useful to Gulf Island travellers.

Camping and Accommodation — Be Prepared

The camping season on the Gulf Islands generally begins around Easter weekend, but some diehards camp year-round. Provincial campgrounds operate on a first-come, first-served basis and a fee is charged in most parks during summer. The number of provincial campsites on the Gulf Islands is inadequate: campers who dawdle when all the other ferry passengers have gone to claim a campsite are frequently disappointed or,

Camping at Montague Harbour.

worse, marooned with nowhere to stay. Set up camp before exploring the island.

Some commercial accommodations provide campsites, often with showers and RV hookups, and they may take reservations. Most are listed in Tourism B.C.'s *Accommodations* booklet.

Finding accommodation in the Gulf Islands in the height of the tourist season is not easy. Although there are many resorts, hotels, motels, lodges, and bed-and-breakfast establishments, the demand for them is high. Reservations are essential during summer and, with growing winter tourism, it's wise to book ahead at all times of year, particularly on holiday weekends.

Accommodations, like other businesses, change and it's impossible to provide up-to-date information in this book. The most reliable source for current accommodation listings, with descriptions of services and rates, is Tourism B.C.'s *Accommodations* booklet, which has been published annually since 1925. About a million copies a year are printed and distributed to three dozen countries. Each accommodation listed in the booklet has been inspected by government "accommodation counsellors" who ensure the particular accommodation meets the government's standards of "comfort, courtesy and cleanliness." Those which meet the standards are given a bright blue "Approved Accommodation" sign or window decal for public display. If a resort, motel, hotel, lodge, or campground is not listed in the guide, it may not be up to standard: when booking a place to stay, ask if the outlet is listed in the guide, and if not, why. Some accommodations may not be listed because they are new, the proprietors failed to submit the nominal listing fee before the publication deadline, or the owner opted to be excluded.

Accommodations is available free from Travel Infocentres throughout British Columbia, from government agent's offices, from travel agents and from the B.C. Ministry of Tourism.

Police and Medical Services on the Gulf Islands

In an emergency on the Gulf Islands get to a phone and dial 911.

The Royal Canadian Mounted Police enforce laws on the Gulf Islands. Permanent detachments on Saltspring and North Pender islands are responsible for the other islands. They patrol both the roads and the waters of the islands.

When island populations explode at the end of the school year, the odd unfortunate incident involving the police and misinformed travellers inevitably occurs. The islands are mistakenly viewed by a flippant few as lawless havens for alcoholic benders. Liquor is the main ingredient of most police problems on the islands and those who abuse it occasionally enjoy an evening of sobering government hospitality.

Lady Minto Gulf Islands Hospital is located on Saltspring, and some islands have medical clinics.

Dogs — Keep Them in Sight

With growing populations, both permanent and visiting, on the Gulf Islands, dogs running loose are a growing problem. Dog owners have a responsibility to respect the rights of individuals who aren't dog lovers: dogs must be kept leashed in public places, particularly parks, population centres, busy streets, hiking trails and beaches. For some people, especially small children, there's nothing more terrifying than a strange dog bounding up as if to offer a friendly greeting. Simply saying, "Oh, he won't bite," isn't good enough: allowing a dog to scare youngsters just spoils someone else's hike on a trail or afternoon on a beach. Dog owners are also expected to clean up feces left by their pets.

Another serious problem with dogs on the Gulf Islands involves sheep and other domestic animals. Once or twice a year there are reports of unfortunate clashes between irresponsible dog owners and farmers who have exercised their right to destroy a dog which has attacked or threatened farm animals. A farmer has the legal right to kill a dog if the dog harms or worries the farmer's livestock: while most farmers are reluctant to kill someone's beloved family pet, they do not hesitate if necessary. There are several sheep farms on the islands and farm animals are not always fenced. Sheep are a prime target for marauding dogs, and every year a few dogs receive the ultimate punishment for their owners' irresponsibility.

Bicycling — The Deceptive Country Road

If the topography of the Gulf Islands could be described in two words, they'd be "kinda lumpy." None of the islands described in this book is hill-free cycling territory: in fact, as far as cycling goes, it would be safe to consider the Gulf Islands a good place to sell rechargeable pacemakers. Some cyclists say 60 kilometres on a Gulf Island is like 90 kilometres anywhere else.

These hills, however, are not insurmountable, especially for regular riders. Literally thousands of cyclists wheel their bikes aboard B.C. ferries each year to tour the islands. Some carry camping gear and set up bases at provincial parks. Others catch early morning sailings, ride for the day and return at sunset. And there are bicycle tour companies, many from the United States, which provide copies of *The Gulf Islands Explorer* as part of their package. With careful study of ferry schedules, you can plan island-hopping trips, setting up new camps at each island or establishing a base camp on one island for day trips to other islands. Combining cycling with bed-and-breakfast stops is popular among riders who don't want to carry camping gear.

The motorists' routes described in this book are equally attractive to bicyclists. Only a few routes, like the dirt roads on Saltspring's mountainous south end, require a mountain bike (and oversized lungs). Cyclists who follow the main routes laid out at the start of each chapter have the obvious advantage of absorbing the island scenery at a more leisurely pace than the motorist.

The campground for boaters and bicyclists at Montague Harbour Park on Galiano, and the walk-in campsites at Ruckle Park, on Saltspring's Beaver Point, are enticing to cyclists because cars can't get there. Like other island roads, the route to Beaver Point requires some endurance, but it's only 10 kilometres from the Fulford Harbour ferry terminal and a good destination for groups of cycling youngsters.

Although some Gulf Island roads appear to be quiet country lanes, many are major thoroughfares, shared by a variety of vehicles from mopeds to logging trucks. Because of the topography of the islands, many roads are tortuous with hills and blind spots, places where loaded logging or dump trucks are unable to stop without warning.

With the growing interest in Gulf Island cycling, there's an increase in complaints from islanders who encounter careless cyclists. Common complaints are cyclists riding four abreast down both sides of the highway, leashed dogs running alongside bicycles, large groups of cyclists congregating near the crests of hills or on blind corners, and, believe it or not, people stopping to pick blackberries and dumping their bicycles in the middle of the road.

It is easy to be deceived by the moderate pace on the Gulf Islands, but travellers should remember that not everyone here is on holiday. The islanders are using the roads to go about their daily business. The last thing they want is to run down a careless cyclist or flatten a bike absent-mindedly parked in the middle of the road: it would ruin their day, and ruin your ride.

All of the amenities required by Gulf Island cyclists are described in this book, along with the routes and maps to get you there. Don't forget to pack it.

Fishing the Gulf Islands — How to Find 'Em, Catch 'Em and Cook 'Em

The most savoury delicacies of the sea are those alive with a freshness known only to those who catch their own. The enviable privilege of landing a trophy-sized chinook or coho salmon is enjoyed in British Columbia by thousands of saltwater anglers. Gulf Island waters are renowned throughout North America for their fighting salmon, lunker bottomfish and fine-tasting shellfish.

Salmon fishing in Georgia Strait is a year-round sport with the best fishing, in some areas, in the dead of winter. Winter spring salmon in the

The author with 16-pound coho.

15- to 30-pound category are commonly taken by anglers courageous enough to challenge the choppy seas and sudden squalls. Good-sized springs and tireless cohoes, however, can be caught in the calmer months, with encouraging spring salmon returns from late April and May until September. Jacksprings, or small chinooks, generally start to show around the end of March and become more plentiful as the weather warms.

Most of the fish moving through the Gulf Islands come up from Juan de Fuca Strait or down through Johnstone Strait to spawn in the Fraser River or rivers along the east side of Vancouver Island. They follow the feed through the channels among the islands and generally appear in the same places at the same time each year. Winter springs usually linger around typically good feeding areas throughout the year and start moving toward the river mouths in September. Some knowledge of overall salmon movements might help visiting anglers hook a prize salmon, but detailed advice should be sought from local fishermen and marina operators. The hottest spots in the Gulf Islands are East Point, Active Pass, Porlier Pass, Sansum Narrows and Thrasher Rock. Anyone fishing or boating in the islands should carry a compass and a set of four charts produced by the Canadian Hydrograhic Service entitled *Gulf Islands — Victoria Harbour to Nanaimo Harbour*. Chart number for the set is 3310.

Licences to fish all "fin fish," including salmon and bottomfish, in tidal waters were introduced in 1981 and regulations should be checked before going fishing. The federal government publishes annually a brochure entitled *British Columbia Tidal Waters Sport Fishing Guide* which outlines laws concerning size and catch limits for salmon, bottomfish and shellfish. The brochure also explains licensing laws including regulations regarding the licensing of boats brought into the country by non-residents to be used for fishing. The brochure is available from sporting goods and tackle shops or marinas. *The Canadian Tide and Current Tables* are also necessary for anglers.

Like any fishing, salmon fishing changes with the tides and days. If it's slow, fishing for cod and other bottomfish may be more productive. Like salmon, bottomfish such as ling cod, red snapper, black bass or sole move about, but not as widely as salmon. Ten minutes of jigging a few centimetres from the bottom is enough to determine the fishiness of a spot. If nothing yanks at your lure, move about 15 metres and try again. Try around kelp beds, rocky bluffs and reefs for bottomfish.

There are several shellfishing beaches throughout the Gulf Islands where people without boats can pick up Dungeness or red rock crabs, oysters, mussels and clams. No licence is required but regulations do apply to shellfish, so check them first.

How to Find the Fish — Read the Water

The angler who dangles his lure over the gunwale and hopes for a strike usually gets skunked. The one who reads the water and fishes the likely spots lands the lunkers.

The days of hit-and-miss salmon fishing are no longer affordable. Without investing at least $100 for basic gear you can't even play the game, and with additional costs for boats, bait and beverage, who can afford to lose? The winners are those who understand something of the elusive salmon's habits, the fishermen who learn to read the water before dropping their tackle over the side.

Reading the water, for some anglers, is glancing around the bay for the greatest concentration of boats and heading over to get in on the action. Tight little groups of boats that gather off points or rocks often begin as one or two boats with no fish and proliferate to a sizeable fleet, with no fish. The highliners, meanwhile, may be sitting in a back eddy, filling their boats with salmon. They follow the fish, not the fishermen.

The most convenient clue to the whereabouts of salmon is surface activity — seabirds and baitfish. Gulls and terns have a habit of noisily advertising their success in locating schools of minnows, particularly when great numbers of herring "ball up" in an effort to escape the jaws of hungry salmon and seabirds. Anglers have been known to drop a buzz bomb into a herring ball, get a good strike, and reel in a glaucous-winged gull.

Birds feeding on the surface indicate schools of baitfish within the top four or five metres. Occasionally baitfish will jump *en masse* or swim right on the surface, giving a momentary impression of raindrops hitting the water.

If there are diving birds — murres or cormorants — feeding with gulls or terns, chances are the fish may be deeper, about 10 or 15 metres. If only diving birds are around, the fish could be as deep as 30 metres.

Finding salmon is more difficult without the help of seabirds, but tide tables and hydrographic charts provide some useful clues. Fish, like people, prefer the path of least resistance, so they rarely linger in the strongest currents. When the tide is running, salmon are likely to be lying on the bottom where the current is slowest. At slack tide they move closer to the surface, especially during periods of low light such as dawn or dusk. Besides telling you the depth, and time of slack tide, charts and tide tables can help you locate back eddies where baitfish and salmon often congregate.

Although points and peninsulas have some effect on tidal direction, tides in Georgia Strait generally flow south on an ebb tide, north on a flood. Back eddies form on the same side of a point, reef or island as the tidal direction. Active Pass, which provides the best summer salmon fishing in the Gulf Islands, is a good example. Anglers, mainly moochers and drift fishermen, fish back eddies near Helen Point at the southwest end of the pass on the ebb tide, and at Georgina Point, on the northeast end, on the flood.

The same principles apply to vertical back eddies which form near reefs or underwater ledges. Find a reef on your chart and if the tide is ebbing, for instance, fish the south side of the reef. If you catch a fish you'll probably want to return to that spot, but don't make the mistake of disregarding the tides. If you fish there on a flood tide next trip, the fish will be on the opposite side of the reef.

Tidelines are often visible on the surface where currents meet. Ripples

Netting the catch.

or rips alongside glass-smooth water, or long streams of bubbles and weed, show where currents meet. As in back eddies, fish are likely to be where the current is weakest, along the edge of the tideline rather than in the middle.

There is no guaranteed method or place to catch salmon. Everyone gets skunked, regardless of expertise. Sometimes the fish just aren't around. Fishing is a fine science and, as all fine scientists know, only a combination of factors working together brings success.

Drift Fishing — Maximum Sport from Minimum Gear

Old fishermen never die, they say, but old fishing methods do, and a growing number of Gulf Island anglers are chucking their heavy trolling rigs in favour of light drift-fishing tackle. Drift fishing, a technique pioneered in local waters, is a back-to-basics way of fishing that gives maximum sport from minimum gear. Not to be confused with drifting rivers for steelhead or trout, drift fishing is precisely what the name implies — fishing from a drifting boat without the objectionable noise and foul fumes of an outboard motor. With light rods and reels and a few weighted lures, drift fishermen working within 10 metres of the surface are finding they can consistently outfish traditional deepwater trollers under the right conditions.

Drift fishing is patterned after simple cod jigging, and although some of the lures are similar to a few used by Scandinavian fishermen, it is a method not widely practised outside the B.C. coast. Well-known local sport fishermen have modified various lures and refined the technique through trial and error. Only in recent years have other anglers begun to see the advantages of drift fishing over heavy weights and flashers.

The equipment is simple: a light, soft-tipped rod about 2.5 to 3.5 metres long, a single-action or spinning reel, a couple of hundred metres of 15- or 20-pound test line, and half a dozen lures. The buzz bomb, created on Vancouver Island, is probably the best-known and oldest drift-fishing lure. Others, such as the stingsilda, deadly dick or pirken, are gaining popularity among Gulf Island sport fishermen.

The methods of fishing all of these lures are basically the same, but the action produced by each differs with the shape and bend of the lure. A buzz bomb, for example, flutters in a spinning motion as it sinks, while a pirken falls more like an oak leaf, at irregular angles. The purpose of the lure is to imitate a crippled baitfish, such as a sandlance, anchovy or herring minnow, and attract lunker spring and coho salmon feeding in and below the schools of baitfish.

Drift-fishing season in Gulf Island waters begins in early spring and summer, when chinooks feed on spawning sandlance in shallow waters, usually less than 30 metres deep. The salmon feed near a sandy bottom and the lure should be worked within a few centimetres of the seabed. In late June and July, herring minnows, averaging about seven or eight centimetres in length, move into shallow bays and hang around anywhere from the surface down to 10 metres.

Spring salmon follow the minnows into shore and feed. Some anglers believe small chinooks feed in the middle of the minnow schools while the big monsters mull around below, gobbling crippled minnows missed by the feeders above. The real action starts in late summer and fall, when mature coho salmon begin moving toward rivers to spawn and mix with the springs. Although cohoes are generally smaller than chinooks, they are frantic feeders and offer more fun per pound than the silvery springs.

There is disagreement among expert anglers about the importance of colour in a lure. While it is advisable to use a lure of colour similar to the bait, it is probably more important to imitate the size of the bait. A lure the same size or slightly larger than the baitfish will produce best results.

When you have selected a spot, tie a one-metre leader to the lure and join it to the line with a swivel. The swivel will prevent the line from twisting as the lure turns in the water. Start within three metres of the surface, gently lifting the rod and then letting the line slacken and the lure flutter down. The salmon will usually hit as the lure falls and the strike may not be immediately apparent. Be careful not to jerk the rod on the upward motion, as the hook could get yanked from the salmon's mouth.

If there is no action near the surface, drop the lure another metre or two, always keeping track of the amount of line you let out so you can duplicate the depth once you have found the fish.

There are times when the water appears to be boiling with life. Baitfish glitter within centimetres of the surface and squawking gulls and terns swoop down to pluck minnows from the sea, hardly making a splash. This is the time for spin casting. Using the same type of lure, cast into the minnow schools and retrieve the lure slowly, pulling the rod tip up and letting the lure drop every few seconds. When a fish hits, give the rod a tug and set the hook. Keep the line taut but set the drag on the reel to let the fish run. A good-sized chinook or coho may take off a dozen times before it is tired enough to net.

The advantages of drift fishing are obvious. It saves energy and allows the fisherman to enjoy the serenity of dawn or dusk on the sea. It is a highly productive method which can be done from rowboats, canoes, docks or rocks and it is simple enough for anyone, regardless of age or experience.

Bucktailing — Watch the Fish Strike

Bucktailing is unquestionably the most exciting way to catch coho salmon. Using light fly rods, mooching reels and flies, fishermen can actually see the salmon strike the lure.

Bucktailing is normally considered an autumn activity, but cohoes can be taken on flies throughout the year. The size of fish and bucktailing methods vary from season to season, but there are few months when a coho cannot be caught within five metres of the surface. The key to successful bucktailing throughout the year is knowing when the cohoes progress from one type of feed to another. In January, February and March, for example, bluebacks — small cohoes up to two and a half pounds — feed near the surface on shrimp. The bluebacks in Georgia Strait waters are a mixture of semi-resident schools and migratory cohoes that spend much of their first year in the gulf. They can be taken near islands and inlet mouths on bushy bucktails about six to eight centimetres long with tinges of orange, pink, red or yellow in the body. Small metal spinners can be attached to the flies, which should be trolled quickly about 22 to 30 metres behind the boat, on the surface or slightly below.

By late spring and summer, these young cohoes are feeding on small baitfish such as sandlance or minnows, and are attracted to sleeker bucktails, usually seven to nine centimetres in length with blue or green tops over white undersides. These salmon can be caught throughout the summer. They like a slower troll with a short line, often so short that the fly sits in the wake of the boat.

Mature autumn cohoes are generally three-year-olds returning to the rivers to spawn and they are looking for larger bucktails — 12 to 18 centimetres — with darker bodies. An abalone or pearl-coloured spinner attached to the fly gives it a wiggle that is irresistible to a hungry coho. These silvery salmon, weighing up to 20 pounds, like a quick troll but they are easily spooked, so the fly should be trolled a good distance from the boat, 45 to 60 metres.

The excitement of bucktailing borders on madness at times. In the midst of a feeding frenzy, birds diving at baitfish and bucktails, salmon leaping on all sides of the boat, the angler's primary problem is staying cool enough to make split-second decisions which mean winning or losing. Some beginners mistakenly believe a coho will strike a bucktail only once and if it is not hooked the first time you just have to wait for another to accept your offer. But a coho can be enticed to strike two or three times after the initial attack if a few metres of line are quickly stripped out after the strike.

It is a common error to pull the rod away from the fish after it hits, as you would to set the hook when drift fishing or trolling. But when bucktailing, only after a coho lightly sets the hook itself should you sink the barb with a good yank.

Locating the fish is something that requires practice, and feeding birds are usually the best bet. If no birds are visible, chances are the fish have moved on or dropped into deeper water. Cohoes also move about within an area. The main school might be feeding near one point when you begin fishing, but 15 or 20 minutes later they could be 100 to 200 metres from that spot. Keep moving until you encounter the fish and circle over and over that spot until they quit biting. Then watch for feeding birds and jumpers and follow them.

Trolling — The Old Standby

Trolling is the traditional method of catching salmon in the Gulf Islands, and while some anglers are switching to techniques requiring lighter gear, others believe trolling remains the most productive. Trolling is undoubtedly the best way to get big winter chinooks which linger near the bottom in water up to 90 metres deep. Some of these monsters weigh up to 40 pounds and many fishermen are willing to tolerate the inconvenience of heavy tackle to hook into trophy-sized salmon.

Trolling equipment varies from simple monofilament lines and weights to downriggers and planers. A downrigger is a manually operated gurdy designed exclusively for sport fishing here on the B.C. coast. While it allows an angler to get the lure within centimetres of a deep bottom, it requires some expertise to use. Some anglers use wire line and a planer, a flat device which dives to the depths, taking the lure with it. Although it is not as complicated as a downrigger, it requires getting used to and can be used only with an extremely heavy rod and line.

The simplest tackle is a fairly stiff rod with a single-action reel, about 300 metres of 30-pound-test monofilament line, and a few lead weights up to two pounds. The weight takes the lure into deep water, but a disadvantage is that it must be hauled up each time the line is checked. This can be hard on the biceps if there is a lot of debris in the water and lines must be checked frequently. A 12- or 16-ounce weight, however, is barely noticeable if you are battling a 20-pound spring salmon.

Lures vary with the time and place and local anglers or marina operators are the best bet for that kind of information. Whether you are using a downrigger, planer or lead weights, there are a few basics to trolling which seasoned trollers use.

Once you have selected the general area to fish, there is some trial and error at the outset. If you are fishing with two lines, it is wisest to put a different lure on each line and lower them to different depths. If both anglers are using one pound of weight, for example, one should strip out about 40 metres of line while the other strips out 60. If you have no success, vary the depths before switching the other lures.

Trolling speeds should also be varied. The action of a lure should always be checked alongside the boat before lowering it. You might find the speed of the boat must be adjusted to get the right movement in the lure. After the tackle is in the water, trolling speeds should be decreased or increased periodically if there is no fishing action.

Trolling, like drift fishing or bucktailing, requires patience and practice.

Shellfish Collectors Beware of Red Tides

In 1943 the federal government established a program to monitor the toxicity of shellfish, caused by red tides. This deadly phenomenon comes from microscopic, single-celled algae that produce some of the most potent natural poisons in the world. Filter-feeding shellfish, such as mussels, oysters or clams, are insensitive to the poisons and accumulate them in their digestive glands. People and other warm-blooded animals, however, can die from ingesting the poisons. Crabs, prawns or shrimp do not accumulate these toxins.

As these algae drift about in surface waters, utilizing sunlight for growth, they go through cycles and multiply many times. When a "bloom" occurs, wind and current conditions may force the algae to concentrate in small areas. Many of these tiny organisms are a reddish colour, and when they concentrate they give the ocean a tomato-soup appearance.

When people and other animals consume shellfish that have ingested the algae, the toxins inhibit the transmission of nerve impulses, causing muscular paralysis and possible death by asphyxiation — a syndrome called paralytic shellfish poisoning. People who eat contaminated shellfish may feel a tingling in their lips and tongue; their fingertips and toes may become numb, and finally they'll lose muscle control. Vomiting should be induced and a doctor should be called.

Under the federal government's monitoring program, samples are collected from shellfish and tested. If toxicity levels exceed certain limits the shellfish area is closed to harvesting and signs are posted to warn people. Some bans remain in effect for several months, even years, and it is both illegal and dangerous to disregard them.

Testing is also done for other shellfish contamination, usually where high fecal coliform counts are suspected. Faulty septic fields are the main cause of fecal contamination in shellfish, and the harvesting of shellfish may be banned around waterfront residential areas. These areas are also signposted.

Now You've Caught 'Em, Time to Cook 'Em

No explanation of Gulf Island fishing would be complete without a few suggestions for the trout and seafood gourmet on preparation of the catch. Here are some simple cooking ideas requiring minimal ingredients for delicious feasts by campfire. The freshness and flavour of a boated fish can be preserved all day by killing the fish immediately and keeping it cool, out of the sun. It should be cleaned as soon as possible by slitting it down the belly, removing the contents and washing the body cavity. The gills should be removed, as they decompose quickly, and the fish wrapped in wet paper, damp burlap, green ferns or moss — not plastic bags.

Salmon and Trout

After cleaning the fish, run the tip of a sharp knife along the inside edge of the backbone, cutting through the bone just enough to spread the fish open on a grill. Spread the fish skin-down over a grill and sprinkle pepper, dill and parsley over the flesh. Spread a thin layer of butter over the fish and lay a few lemon slices on the top. The fire should be burned down, leaving enough hot coals to cook for about half an hour. Lean the grill against a rock or a couple of sticks, about 30 centimetres from the coals, allowing the fish to cook slowly, without turning, until the bones can be pulled away easily from the cooked flesh.

If a grill isn't handy, the same ingredients can be used to cook the fish in a frying pan or wrapped in aluminum foil. After the fish is cleaned, leave the two sides attached to the backbone and stuff the body cavity with lemon slices and mushrooms. Cover the fish in aluminum foil or lay it in a frying pan and put it over the coals near the edge of the fire. About 10 minutes per side is normal cooking time. If the fish flakes when poked with a fork, your gourmet dish is ready for the taste test.

Bottomfish

Cod or sole fillets can be seasoned, like salmon or trout, with pepper, spices, butter and lemon. They can be placed in aluminum foil or a frying pan and cooked over hot coals for about five minutes per side. Steaming cod, however, helps maintain the firmness, making the fish slightly easier to handle when you are working by a beach fire without the convenient utensils of home. A makeshift steamer can be made by wedging thin sticks between the sides of a saucepan or pot to keep the fish sitting above the water. Boil saltwater over hot coals and place the fillets, with the skin removed, on the sticks. Cover the pot and cook the ingredients for about 15 minutes. Add the spices and lemon juice when it's cooked.

Dungeness Crab

Most seafood gourmets argue that crab, like Atlantic lobster, should be cooked live. As crab meat deteriorates quickly, it is essential to keep a crab alive until it is time to plop it into the pot. But why boil up all that excess gunk when your only interest is the sweet, solid meat inside the legs, pinchers and body? While you are waiting for a pot of seawater to boil, take the crab to the beach and deliver the *coup de grâce*.

To do this, point the crab away from your body and grasp all the legs and pinchers from below the body with the palms of your hands facing up. Once you've got a good grip on the beast, the pinchers offer no defence. Find a hard, narrow surface, like the edge of a bucket or board, and give the crab a hard swack to lift off the top of the shell. Break the crab in half and chuck the slimy entrails to the squawking assemblage of seagulls that gathered in anticipation when they saw what you were up to. Swish the two halves around in the ocean and drop them into the pot.

Overcooking is the most common method of turning luscious, firm crab meat into a watery mass of mush. Ten minutes will do. There are countless sauces in which to dip the little chunks of meat, but the only way to experience the true taste of west coast Dungeness crab is to eat it straight out of the shell.

Clams

With the exception of oysters, which can be eaten raw, clams are probably the easiest seafood to prepare. Simply drop them into a pot of boiling seawater and cook them until the shells open, usually only a few minutes. They can also be steamed open, rinsed and eaten. The squishy green substance, which you'll find when you take the clam out of the shell, should be discarded along with the long siphon.

If you have a few vegetables, some spices and dried or canned soup, a delectable clam chowder can be whipped up over a beach fire. After steaming or boiling open the clams, rinse them and put them aside. Discard the seawater in which the clams were boiled. Fry some bacon until it is crisp, chop it up, and sauté a couple of chopped onions in the bacon fat. Chop some potatoes into chunks. Using equal portions of milk and fresh water, make some tomato or onion soup and drop everything into the brew. Season it with pepper, salt and any other available spices, cover the pot and let it simmer for 10 to 15 minutes. You can't buy fresher clam chowder.

Oysters

British Columbia's boldest beachcombers eat raw oysters. They pluck a shell from the beach, shuck it and drop the slippery morsel down the gullet. Those who dangle a naked oyster over their noses a split-second too long usually haul out the seafood cookbook.

Oyster shucking is a procedure that improves with practice but there's a lazy cooking method which eliminates the frustration frequently suffered by amateur shuckers. Just chuck the oysters on hot coals, shell and all, and let them sit until the shells open. Remove the oyster and eat it with a touch of Worcestershire sauce or ketchup.

Shrimpers — The Midnight Fishermen

As the autumn sun sets over the Gulf Islands, small armies of shrimpers prepare to march into the night. Laden with lamps, traps, camp stoves and bait, they converge on marinas, private docks and government

Checking the trap.

wharves to capture the beady-eyed shrimp. They're fishermen-turned-gourmets, willing to withstand nippy November nights for a small taste of fresh seafood.

Shallow-water shrimping in the Gulf Islands is an after-dark pastime that lasts from late August through November and costs next to nothing. And with shrimp meat being among the most expensive local seafood, who can afford to stay indoors when the shrimp are biting?

These tasty little cousins of the crayfish begin feeding around wharves and pilings after sunset and keep eating until after midnight. They seem to arrive in waves, or surges, and shrimpers often pull full traps every 10 or 15 minutes for an hour or so; then their luck tapers off for a while until another wave of shrimp moves in.

The equipment is simple and cheap: a flashlight, of course, to see what you are doing; some bait, such as an old fish head, clams or even a can of sardines punched full of holes; and a trap with 10 or 15 metres of line. The trap can be built from old bicycle wheels or any other type of wood or metal hoop about 700 centimetres in diameter. Stretch a burlap sack over the ring to form a shallow basket and tie the rope to four places on the edge of the hoop.

The bait, preferably a fish head which has been left in the open air a couple of days to give it that fragrance that shrimp love, should be tied or wired to the centre of the trap. Secure the end of the line to the wharf, lower the trap into the murky depths, and put your feet up while the shrimp descend upon the bait. As you slowly retrieve the trap you will likely see the glowing eyes of dozens of shrimp, like phosphorescent beads glued to their spiny heads. Keep them fresh in a bucket of saltwater until you have enough to fire up the camp stove.

Most experienced shrimpers catch, clean and cook the shrimp right on the wharf, so while someone is minding the traps, someone else is playing seafood chef, and others are gobbling shrimp. If you are catching a lot of shrimp, some type of beverage is important to wash them down.

Shrimp should be boiled in seawater and left to cool naturally in the open air. Much of the flavour is lost if they are rinsed in cold, fresh water. Some seasoned shrimpers believe an extra dash of salt in the boiling water helps bring out the flavour. They should be cooked only two or three minutes — until they turn bright red. Overcooking makes the meat mushy and difficult to extract from the tail.

After the shrimp is cooked, snap off the head and squeeze the tail, forcing the meat out. Some seafood epicures keep a sauce handy — mayonnaise and ketchup with a touch of horseradish — to dip the meat into before popping it onto the taste buds.

The type of shrimp most commonly caught in shallow waters around the Gulf Islands is coon-stripe shrimp between seven and 15 centimetres long. Shrimp are crustaceans, not bivalves like clams or oysters, and are therefore not dangerous or illegal to catch and eat in areas where shellfish-harvesting bans are imposed.

Many wharves or docks are not well-illuminated, so shrimpers would be wise to wear lifejackets. When you are preoccupied with nets, bait, shrimp and camp stoves, it is easy to step back a pace and disappear between two floats. If you are wearing a flotation device you will bob up like a cork; if you are not, you might be swallowed by the darkness.

Active Pass —
A Unique and Controversial Waterway

Millions of passengers aboard B.C. ferries travel through Active Pass every year, and while most are struck by the spectacular scenery as the ship winds its way between Galiano and Mayne Island, a few are aware of the significance of this fascinating channel as a wildlife sanctuary, a major transportation route, and a prized salmon-fishing ground. Active Pass is the busiest waterway in the Gulf Islands, used by a variety of vessels including ferries, freighters, fishboats, pleasure boats, and sport-fishing boats.

ACTIVE PASS

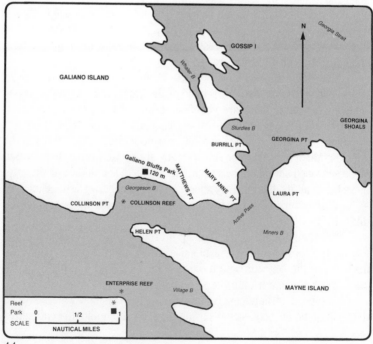

Its importance as a wildlife sanctuary is recognized across Canada. Up to 7,000 Brandt cormorants winter in the pass, 10,000 Pacific loons move through in spring, and an estimated 10,000 Bonaparte gulls feed on schools of herring in the turbulent waters. In late winter or early spring, passengers aboard ferries in the pass have counted as many as 70 bald eagles at a time. A dozen or so northern, or Steller's, sea lions often linger around Helen Point and Collinson Reef, near the southwest entrance to the pass, in winter. Porpoises frequently swim through the pass, and nomadic pods of killer whales are occasionally spotted outside either entrance. Once in a while the whales swim through the pass.

The waters of Active Pass provide the best summer salmon fishing in the Gulf Islands, and anglers from both sides of Georgia Strait congregate off the points at either end of the pass every day throughout summer. As many as 60 small boats can be seen drifting off Helen Point on the ebb tide or Georgina Point on the flood, as anglers test their skills on the chinook and coho salmon feeding off the points.

This excellent fishing, however, occurs during months when ferry traffic is highest, and fears of a collision between fishermen and ferries have been expressed repeatedly since the mid-1960s. Nearly half of the passengers who travel through the pass aboard the ferries each year are carried during June, July and August, when salmon fishing is at its peak.

In August 1970, the Russian freighter *Sergey Yesenin* collided with the ferry *Queen of Victoria* near Collinson Point at the southwest entrance to the pass. Three people were killed. In August 1979, the ferry *Queen of Alberni* ran aground on Collinson Reef, causing an estimated $1,250,000 damage. A cry of "ban the boaters" resounded through the pass after each

Ferry and fisherman in Active Pass.

45

incident, but subsequent investigations absolved pleasure boaters and sport fishermen of any blame.

The 1979 grounding, however, brought the long-simmering ferries-versus-fishermen feud to a boil, and the Canadian government ordered public meetings to bring all the facts about Active Pass on deck. The B.C. Ferry Corporation asked for an outright ban on all sport fishing in Active Pass, while sport fishermen asked for changes in operating methods of the ferries. The result was a juggling of ferry schedules, to reduce chances of ferries meeting one another in the pass, and beefed-up RCMP enforcement of small-boating regulations.

The natural characteristics of Active Pass form the basis of the controversy. The tidal flows which provide the excellent salmon fishing also make Active Pass a dangerous waterway, regardless of the marine traffic. The highest volume of water in any Gulf Island channel flows through Active Pass, as much as 750,000 cubic metres per minute at certain times. The phenomenal flow has a profound effect on marine life, fishing, and manoeuvrability of vessels, regardless of size.

The pass, precisely midway between Vancouver Island and the lower mainland, stretches 5.5 kilometres from the northeast entrance, which faces onto Georgia Strait, to the southwest entrance, between Helen and Collinson points. Distance across the pass varies from about 550 metres at three places to approximately 1,700 metres between Sturdies Bay on Galiano and Georgina Point on Mayne. It is almost S-shaped, with 90-degree turns at the approaches to both ends.

The tide floods toward Georgina Point and if strong winds blow in the opposite direction to the tidal flow, rip tides form. Steep waves remain stationary, taking a long time to dissipate and building in height. Wash from the ferries also combines with flood tides at the other end of the pass to form steep rips. Waves get trapped across the narrowest part of the pass and sit in mid-channel for an hour at a time. Small boats are occasionally swamped attempting to cross the rip tides.

The ebb tide at the southwest entrance creates back eddies outside Helen Point and along stretches of shoreline inside the pass. These back eddies provide good fishing and safe areas for small craft to travel. Highest tidal velocities off Helen Point are eight knots, and while undertows have little effect on shallow-draught boats, they can cause a sailboat to list up to 30 degrees.

Two resident schools of mature herring concentrate in the back eddies at Helen Point on the ebb tide and at Georgina Point on the flood. The herring attract the salmon which, in turn, attract the fishermen. The pass is a crossroads for salmon returning to spawn in the Fraser River, which has the world's largest natural salmon runs, the Cowichan River, and other streams in B.C. and the United States.

Near-collisions between ferries and sport fishermen have occurred during summer at various places, but the main trouble spot is Helen Point. Many of the boaters fishing off the point drift in the back eddies with their engines shut off. The main back eddy is just outside the point and as the tide slackens and begins to turn, drifting boats are carried across the entrance to the channel. A minority of those boaters ignore ferries bearing down on them at 18 knots and refuse to move off the collision course until the last moment. RCMP officers have even encountered anglers, playing fish, who ask police to radio ferry captains with requests to alter course or slow down until the fish are landed.

There are several good viewpoints over Active Pass on Mayne and Galiano islands which are mentioned in the chapters on those islands. You could easily spend an entire afternoon watching the wildlife and marine traffic through binoculars from a number of places.

If you hear a long, single blast from a ship's horn, you can expect the blue and white bow of a B.C. ferry to appear around a point within moments. If you hear five short blasts, someone is on a collision course with the signalling ferry.

The Gulf Islands — A Yachtman's Paradise

The Gulf Islands are easily accessible to pleasure boaters from both sides of Georgia Strait and both sides of the Canadian-American border. Cruising guides and atlases that detail coves and anchorages on most of the islands are available for Gulf Island boaters.

There are government wharves on all Gulf Islands, and many have

Author's wife prepares for summer sailing.

47

marinas. This book offers suggestions for walks and other activities near areas where boaters are likely to anchor or moor their vessels.

The conscientious yachtsman, naturally, is expected to already be aware of weather patterns and tides and be equipped with proper sounding gear and charts. This book does not, therefore, detail locations of rocks and reefs or provide information which is normally carried by pleasure boaters.

Canoeing, Kayaking and Small Boating in the Gulf Islands

The sheltered waters of the Gulf Islands are among the finest in the world for touring in small boats. Tidal currents are usually harmless, crossings are short, and beaches are plentiful if there is a need to pull out. With basic equipment, a little local knowledge and common sense, there are few places in the Gulf Islands that cannot be seen from a small boat.

There is little difference in operating a small boat on the sea or on a lake, but people unaccustomed to ocean travel should be aware of a few things. Distances between islands and across large bays can be deceiving, and it is safer to check a chart for an accurate distance than to guess by looking over the water. Get used to estimating the time necessary to make crossings and, whenever possible, take the shortest crossing.

Winds come up quickly, often in 10 or 15 minutes, in the Gulf Islands, as they do on large interior lakes. Narrow channels and steep bluffs can have a local effect on winds, making them gusty and dangerous if there

Harbour seals.

48

is nowhere to pull out. Winds can be spotted in many places throughout the islands before they actually arrive at your location. Keep an eye ahead and over your shoulder for a darkening on the surface of the water or clouds which appear to be moving toward you. Allow ample time to get to a sheltered shore and wait out any unexpected squalls.

Tides are often puzzling to people who normally travel on fresh water. *The Canadian Tide and Current Tables* explain tide and current movements, but many people who are used to boating on lakes forget to pull their vessels high enough up the beach before leaving them for some time. Light boats should always be packed up to the logs and tied to something stationary to avoid the possibility of getting stranded. Even if you are going for a half-hour stroll, it is wise to fasten the bowline to something secure before leaving the boat.

Late summer and fall is the best canoeing time in the islands because of morning and evening calms. You can get an early start, beach the boat for an afternoon of exploring, and put in a couple of hours before bunking down on a beach. It is also coho season and a bucktail dragged a few metres astern often snags a snack for an evening campfire.

Tidal currents in the Gulf Islands usually run about one or two knots

Whiskery snout of river otter.

and can be used to the advantage of slow boaters. Generally, tides ebb south and flood north, so a trip can be planned to run with the flow. There are a few places, such as Active Pass or Porlier Pass, which should be avoided by canoeists because of extremely strong and hazardous tides and insufficient time to traverse them at slack tide. Only highly experienced paddlers should tackle those waters. *Canadian Tide and Current Tables, Volume 5*, entitled *Juan de Fuca and Georgia Straits*, is essential equipment for Gulf Island ocean travel.

The Canadian Hydrographic Service also produces a *Small Craft Guide* and a set of four charts, entitled *Gulf Islands — Victoria Harbour to Nanaimo Harbour* which, with a compass, is necessary for island navigation. The set, number 3310, is packaged in a folder with illustrations of fundamental chart symbols and nautical distances between Gulf Island points. A basic understanding of these charts will not only help you plot your course, but will show the type of shoreline and terrain you can expect to encounter.

Fresh water in the Gulf Islands is not plentiful during summer and it is advisable to pack your own. A sun hat is also a good idea, as a combination of direct sun and salt air can cause sunburn and sunstroke.

Thanks to the mild climate of the Gulf Islands, a tent is usually excess baggage. A good-sized tarp with thin foam mattress and sleeping bag is sufficient gear for a comfortable night's sleep on some out-of-the-way beach. During summer a tarp may be unnecessary. Best camping facilities are at provincial marine parks, but it is not against the law to camp on crown land, such as a beach.

Paddling and small boating in the Gulf Islands do not need to be confined to summer and early fall. Although the winds are stronger and rains heavier during winter, there are still many pleasant journeys to be made in the so-called off-season. A trip to Beaumont Marine Park on South Pender, a tour of Montague Harbour on Galiano, or a circumnavigation of the Chain Islands in Ganges Harbour are a few.

A Word about the Metric System

Canada's metric system is often confusing to people unaccustomed to dealing with it but fairly easy to live with once you get used to it. Simple conversions, such as inches to centimetres, miles to kilometres, or acres to hectares, present little problem when you know the multiplication factors. This book conforms to the metric system with a few exceptions.

Ocean distances shown in various sections remain in nautical miles rather than kilometres. A nautical mile is longer than a land mile and cannot be converted easily to kilometres. More important, the Canadian

Hydrographic Service produces charts for mariners which show distances in nautical miles and there are no immediate plans to switch those distances to kilometres.

Secondly, a fisherman used to weighing a fish in pounds will probably never get used to referring to the weight in kilograms. If it is suggested to you that chances of catching a 4.5-kilogram salmon in the Gulf Islands are good, do you visualize yourself proudly standing before the camera, holding a 10-pound chinook or coho? Besides difficulty in imagining the size of a fish under metric measurement, the phrase "4.5-kilogrammer" doesn't roll off the tongue as smoothly, or as smugly, as "ten-pounder."

Here is a simple table to help you understand the metric system:

When you know	Multiply by	To find
centimetres	.4	inches
metres	3.3	feet
kilometres	.63	miles
square metres	1.25	square yards
square kilometres	.4	square miles
hectares	2.5	acres
kilograms	2.2	pounds

Or:

inches	2.5	centimetres
feet	.3	metres
miles	1.6	kilometres
square yards	.8	square metres
square miles	2.6	square kilometres
acres	.4	hectares
pounds	.45	kilograms

Temperatures are given in Celsius and their relationship to the Fahrenheit scale is shown on the following page.

Fahrenheit/Celsius

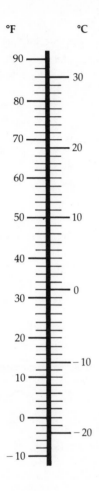

Saltspring Island

Diverse and Populated

 Saltspring is the largest and most populated of all the islands in the Gulf of Georgia. With 180 square kilometres and some 8,000 inhabitants, it is more than three times the size of Galiano, the second-largest Gulf Island, and accommodates more than half of the total population of the islands. It is remarkably diverse, having mountain peaks of nearly 700 metres, secluded cutthroat streams, a dozen trout and bass lakes, and an estimated 640 kilometres of roads.

Saltspring's name originates from an unusual phenomenon on the island's north end — 14 springs of brine, varying in size from a metre to as much as 25 metres in diameter. Salt crystals around these springs

53

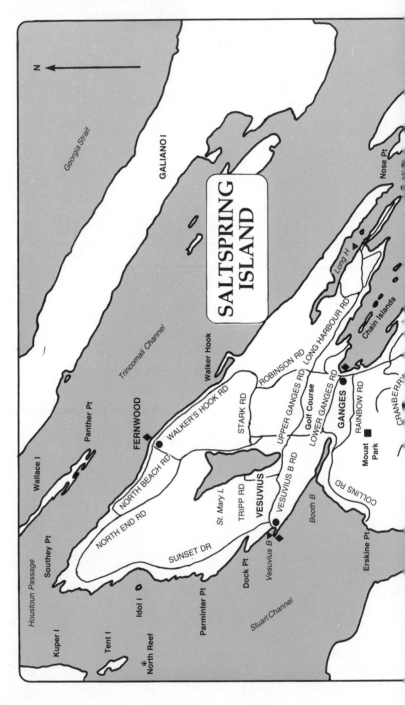

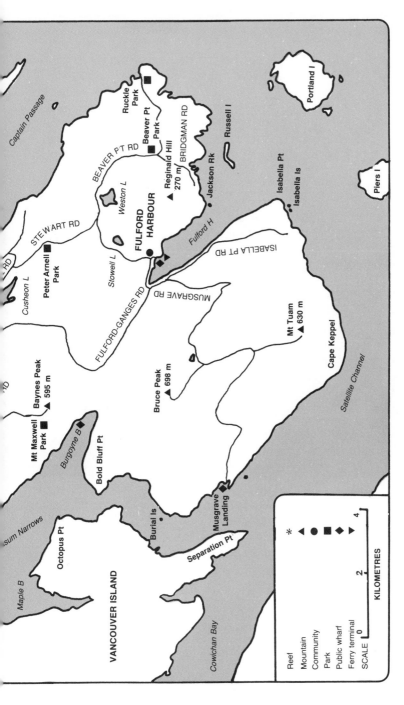

Captain Passage

Portland I

Ruckle Park

Beaver Pt Park

Russell I

BEAVER PT RD

BRIDGMAN RD

Reginald Hill
▲ 270 m

Jackson Rk

Isabella Pt

Isabella Is

Weston L

STEWART RD

FULFORD HARBOUR

Fulford H

Peter Arnell Park

Stowell L

Cusheon L

ISABELLA PT RD

FULFORD-GANGES RD

MUSGRAVE RD

Mt Tuam
▲ 630 m

Cape Keppel

Satellite Channel

Baynes Peak
▲ 595 m

Mt Maxwell Park

Burgoyne B

Bold Bluff Pt

Bruce Peak
▲ 698 m

Maple B

sum Narrows

Octopus Pt

Burial Is

Musgrave Landing

Separation Pt

VANCOUVER ISLAND

Cowichan Bay

Piers I

Reef   *
Mountain   ◄
Community   ●
Park   ■
Public wharf ◆
Ferry terminal ►

SCALE 0   2   4
      KILOMETRES

55

glitter in the sunlight and the only vegetation in the immediate vicinity is a strange species of grass and a tiny, pink flower, known as sea blush, which grows on the edge of the springs. Sometimes bubbles unexpectedly break the surface of the springs, which are located on private property. Saltspring is the only Gulf Island with salt springs.

Geologically, Saltspring is divided into three distinctly separate sections. The rugged and mountainous south end, which includes Mount Tuam and Bruce Peak, is separated from the middle of the island by the Fulford Valley, which runs between Burgoyne Bay and Fulford Harbour. The middle of the island, which is also mountainous, especially on the south and southwest sides, is cut off from the top of the island by a two-kilometre valley connecting Booth Inlet with Ganges Harbour. The north end of Saltspring is also the low end, with fewer high peaks and more rolling pasture land and deciduous forests.

It is at this end that most of Saltspring's people live, between Ganges and Southey Point. Residential development seems to be spreading out from Ganges, with new subdivisions on both sides of the village. There are small communities around St. Mary Lake, at Fernwood, at Vesuvius Bay and in the Long Harbour area. Although there are homes at Cusheon Lake and at various places throughout the region between Ganges and Fulford Harbour, Fulford is the only concentrated population centre south of Ganges.

The isolation of this intriguing island is as remarkable as its diversity when one considers that British Columbia's capital city is less than an hour away and Canada's third-largest city can be reached by car and ferry within two hours. Yet the unanxious lifestyle in communities like Fulford Harbour, Vesuvius Bay or Fernwood is immediately recognized by newcomers.

Saltspring, because of its proximity to Victoria and easy accessibility from both sides of Georgia Strait, is a good starting point for expeditions to the outer islands. Many people visiting Saltspring for the first time, however, are so enthralled that they never make it to the other islands. From ferry terminals at Fulford Harbour, Vesuvius Bay or Long Harbour, a driver can take a 60-kilometre whirlwind tour and cover the island in less than two hours, but a holiday of hiking, fishing, boating, beachcombing, bicycling, and sightseeing can last a weekend, a couple of weeks, or forever.

A Route to Follow

Saltspring's diversity becomes apparent to visitors shortly after landing on the island. One minute you can be looking deep into Vancouver Island's Cowichan Valley from a height of more than 600 metres; 15 minutes later you can be lying at sea level in a grassy field watching hang gliders soar over the Fulford Valley. You can take time for a dip in the fresh, warm water of Cusheon Lake or catch a case of goose bumps in the chilly sea at Beddis Beach. You can spend an afternoon playing golf, poking around novelty shops in Ganges or taking a leisurely country stroll on a quiet, north-end road.

A quick trip around the island can begin at any ferry terminal and end at the same point. From Fulford Harbour, for example, take Fulford-Ganges Road to Ganges, drive through the village to Lower Ganges Road, then follow Vesuvius Bay Road to Sunset Drive. Take Sunset Drive to North End Road and at North Beach Road, turn left and drive along the waterfront through Fernwood to Walker Hook. From Walker Hook continue down Robinson Road beyond Long Harbour Road and back through Ganges to Beddis Road. Turn left onto Beddis, drive to Stewart Road and make a right turn. At the end of Stewart Road turn right on Beaver Point Road back to Fulford Harbour.

Through over a dozen journeys off this main route, you will discover awesome views of Mount Baker on the American mainland, secluded coves and shell beaches, picturesque evergreen and deciduous forests with exotic species of twisted Garry oak and arbutus, magnificent seascapes and moss-covered bluffs and rocky headlands.

If you begin at Fulford Harbour, you will immediately encounter St. Paul's Roman Catholic Church, a tiny stone building overlooking the harbour. The church was built between 1880 and 1885 by a young priest named Father Donckele, who was assistant to Father Peter Rondeault. Father Rondeault oversaw the building of the famed Butter Church in Vancouver Island's Cowichan Valley. Building materials from the Butter Church, which bears a striking resemblance to St. Paul's, were ferried in long, Indian war

At rest on shores of Fulford Harbour.

canoes across the often-treacherous waters of Sansum Narrows to Burgoyne Bay. They were then laboriously hauled by stone-boat and oxen through the Fulford Valley to the site of St. Paul's.

The priests in charge of St. Paul's were frequently forced to brave the strong currents and tidal rips of Sansum Narrows to meet their associates in the Cowichan Valley. It was during one of these uncomfortable canoe voyages that a priest named Father Kremers met Skookum Tom, a Gulf Island Indian with seven wives. As it was Father Kremer's duty to Christianize the natives, he was faced with the awkward task of informing Skookum Tom that the Catholic Church permitted only monogamous

St. Paul's Church.

relationships. After lengthy and frustrating discussions, Skookum Tom reluctantly agreed, much to the chagrin of six wives, to keep only his favourite wife and join the church.

As the road moves away from Fulford Harbour, the imposing summits of Bruce Peak and Mount Maxwell loom high above. Up the hill and around a few bends is Blackburn Lake, a tiny lake often visited in summer by pint-sized polliwog hunters. The highway climbs to about 120 metres as you approach Ganges, affording an open view of the Chain Islands in Ganges Harbour, several other Gulf Islands, and mountains on the lower mainland. At the foot of Ganges Hill, in the centre of town, are Centennial Park and the Ganges government wharf, where public washrooms are located near a children's playground. Ganges is described in further detail in the Shopping and Services section of this chapter.

As you leave the village, the distinction between Upper and Lower Ganges roads is somewhat confusing, but either road will take you to Vesuvius Bay Road. A few hundred metres beyond the turnoff to Sunset Drive is Vesuvius Bay, the home of Saltspring's first pioneers. A group of nine Negro slaves, who had purchased their liberty in the United States, arrived at Vesuvius in 1857 and were followed by other blacks, and white people of varying nationalities, before the end of that decade.

The first settlers actually carved homesites out of the dense forests a couple of miles away from shore to hide from the frequent and savage clashes on the beach between Gulf Island Indians and their northern enemies. Island pioneers lived their earlier days under the constant threat of attacks by hostile natives.

The unassuming homes and tidy gardens clustered around a tranquil bay at Vesuvius give this winsome community a maritime aura which makes visitors envious of those who live here. From the beach and docks you can watch tugs and fishboats running through Stuart Channel.

There is some pretty, rolling farmland along Sunset Drive and North End Road, where the odd sheep may stray across the road. As you approach the ocean alongside North Beach Road, you can look across Trincomali Channel to Galiano Island. If you stop to walk on the public wharf or along the shore at Fernwood, you might see the spotted gray head of a nosy harbour seal suddenly pop out of the sea.

After passing Walker Hook and retracing your tracks through Ganges, you will find Beddis Road dropping down along the southwest side of Ganges Harbour for nearly five kilometres before branching right to Stewart Road. Slightly less than one kilometre along Stewart, the road takes a sharp turn to the left where it meets Cusheon Lake Road. About 1.6 kilometres from the turn, Stewart Road curves right at Peter Arnell Park, a local park named for an English-born surveyor who was accidentally shot at the age of 38 while surveying on Galiano Island. A ridge in the park, on which a monument to Peter Arnell has been erected, offers an appropriate view of Galiano.

Once on Beaver Point Road, a short jaunt to the right takes you to Stowell Lake, a popular swimming hole on hot summer days. From Stowell Lake, it is less than three kilometres back to the Fulford ferry terminal.

What the Main Route Misses

Following the same route around Saltspring, there are several side trips which could turn an afternoon's drive into a week-long vacation. All of these excursions can be done by car with minimal walking. Many of the areas described, however, have pleasant walking trails or beaches for those who want to get out and stretch their legs, breathe a bit of fresh sea air, and hear the rush of waves lapping at the shore. The side trips are listed here in the order in which they would be encountered by following the route from Fulford Harbour.

Drummond Park and Fulford Beaches

A short distance up Musgrave Road is Drummond Park, site of a rather controversial Indian petroglyph. The petroglyph, a sandstone carving of a seal, is one of only 500 rock paintings and petroglyphs in British Columbia and is protected under provincial law. It was first found in the water at Fulford Harbour by a local resident and moved to the safety of the beach. The man later moved it to the former Fulford airstrip, where it rested until provincial authorities ordered its removal to a highways yard.

The petroglyph, weighing several tonnes and measuring about two metres in diameter, was finally transported to its current roost in Drummond Park. Historians and local Indians believe it was carved by a Tsaout Indian whose people once inhabited the shores of Fulford Harbour. Indian legend tells us the petroglyph was originally a women who was changed into a rock in order to safeguard the recreation grounds of the Tsaout band.

Directly in front of the park and farther along the road, there are several sand and gravel beaches, excellent areas for rockhounding or collecting unusual driftwood formations.

Burgoyne Bay

There is a public wharf and a log-booming ground at Burgoyne Bay and a beautiful sand beach at the head of the bay, which is easy to reach by foot at low tide. The bay is the site of a private oyster lease, so restrain yourself from collecting any oysters. This bay was once a favourite haunt for cattle rustlers who carried out their devious work under the shelter of night. John Maxwell, who raised Texas longhorn cattle on a 400-hectare farm on the bay, was the repeated victim.

Cusheon Lake

Cusheon Lake, a short jog down Cusheon Lake Road off Fulford-Ganges Road, is a pleasant place for a plunge on an August afternoon.

Mount Maxwell Provincial Park

The best view of the Fulford Valley is from Baynes Peak at the summit of Mount Maxwell. From rock ledges on the peak at 595 metres, you can see the entire valley stretching nearly five kilometres from the head of Burgoyne Bay to Fulford Harbour. On the Fulford side there is a clear view of the smaller Gulf Islands beyond the mouth of the harbour. Maple Bay,

Fulford Valley seen from Mt. Maxwell.

on Vancouver Island, and parts of Sansum Narrows are visible to the west, where boom boats working in Burgoyne Bay look like toys in a miniature world. The sheer drop from the summit has claimed the life of one islander and seriously injured a 13-year-old American boy. Don't venture outside the guard rails.

There are limestone caves decorated with glimmering stalagmites and stalactites on Mount Maxwell's lower ridges, along with three enormous ant hills. Unfortunately, the cave entrances and ant hills are difficult to locate because of the steep climb down the side of the mountain.

A few rusting mufflers lying at the edge of the ten-kilometre road up the mountain are sombre proof of this road's unsuitability for extremely low-slung cars. Condition of the road varies with maintenance, but it is not recommended for large recreational vehicles.

Mount Maxwell, because of its sheer drop on the southwest side, is a launching point for dauntless hang gliders who soar over the Fulford Valley. Watch for them if you're coming into Fulford Harbour aboard a ferry.

Ganges Heights

A steep and winding drive of one kilometre up Charlesworth Road above Ganges takes you to a nice viewpoint over Ganges Harbour. You can pull off the road at a break in the trees for a look directly down to the fishboats at the Ganges public wharf. There are good views of the Chain Islands in the harbour and the islands and mountains beyond Saltspring.

Ganges Beach

At the end of Churchill Road, off Upper Ganges Road, there is access to a small beach facing Goat Island and the Chain Island Group. Although the main facilities of Ganges Harbour are almost immediately adjacent to this beach, it is conveniently tucked behind a point. You can sit on a log and watch the traffic in Ganges Harbour without being a part of the crowd.

Arbutus Beach

The sand and gravel shore of Arbutus Beach, also known as Cranberry Outlet, stretches about 300 metres along the edge of Stuart Channel near Erskine Point on the west side of Saltspring. It is accessible by a 6.4-kilometre drive along Rainbow Road from Ganges, onto Collins Road at the end of Rainbow. Booth Canal Road, off Lower Ganges Road, also leads to Arbutus Beach. There are several old roads near the beach, and Maxwell Creek flows over the beach into the ocean.

Booth Bay

Booth Bay, at the end of Baker Road, is known for its oyster beds and beautiful view of Stuart Channel. A steep, five-metre path from a small parking area at the end of the road leads to the beach, a good spot for evening sun.

Vesuvius Bay

A small beach facing onto Stuart Channel can be reached via a stairway on Langley Street, off Vesuvius Bay Road.

Southey Point

There are tiny coves at the end of Arbutus and Southey Point roads

Long Harbour.

with views of the islands off the end of the point. The Secretary Islands, and Wallace, Jackscrew, Kuper and Tent islands form a V-shaped chain around the northern tip of Saltspring, separated from Southey Point by Houstoun Passage. The islands are so near the point that voices of boaters anchored in the bays can be heard across the channel on a calm day.

St. Mary Lake

St. Mary Lake, Saltspring's major resort area, is the largest body of fresh water in the Gulf Islands. A drive of about five kilometres along North End Road from the junction at North Beach Road takes you to a pull-off area beside the lake, where there is good swimming. Take a short run up Fairway Drive, across from the lake, for a good view of St. Mary Lake.

Long Harbour

Long Harbour is an out-of-the-way part of Saltspring that is better known as a ferry terminal location than a place to explore, but there are a few sites worth checking. En route to the harbour from the intersection of Upper Ganges Road, you will pass Quebec Drive, which leads to a beach near the head of the harbour. A drive of slightly more than one kilometre takes you there. There is a picnic area near the ferry terminal at the end of Long Harbour Road, and several eagle roosts are located on Scott Point Drive.

Beddis Beach

A .8-hectare park on Beddis Beach is located fewer than 7.5 kilometres from Fulford-Ganges Road, at the end of Beddis Road. Broken white shells mixed with fine gravel on the beach give the shoreline a greenish blue, tropical appearance. The beach, although fairly small, is one of the most beautiful on the island, with views of Prevost Island, Captain Passage, North Pender and Swanson Channel.

The beach is situated at the end of a short driveway where Beddis Road swings up to the right and Lionel Crescent runs left off Beddis. The driveway is directly in front of the junction. A parking lot and log outhouse are the only park facilities.

Beaver Point

Beaver Point is one of Saltspring's most intriguing areas, with a history as colourful as the scenery that skirts its shores. Ruckle Provincial Park, with more than 480 hectares on the point, is the largest park in the Gulf

Islands. There are eight coves and bays along its seven kilometres of shoreline, exceptional views of the southern Gulf Islands, and acres of open meadow and evergreen forest. Part of the park is still operated as a farm and sheep or turkeys wander freely along the roads. Many islanders and regular Saltspring visitors believe Beaver Point is the most beautiful corner of the island.

As you drive along Beaver Point Road to the park, you will pass Beaver Point Provincial Park, a 16-hectare park established many years before Ruckle Park. This park, situated at the site of the community hall, is the location of Beaver Point School, which closed its doors in 1951 after educating Saltspring youngsters for 66 years. It is the second-oldest school building still standing in British Columbia.

Across the road from the school is Bridgman Road. This road will take you to a small beach that faces Russell Island at the south end of Saltspring. Weston Lake, known for its lunker-sized trout, is also on Beaver Point Road.

The forests of Beaver Point were once a favoured territory for pit-lampers who would sneak into the woods at night with bicycle lamps and rifles in search of deer. At that time the woods were inhabited by a variety of animals, but the wild animals were not nearly as dangerous as the hunters.

There was one pit-lamper from Texas who claimed he could tell one animal from another by the eyes glowing in the dark. He crept into the forest one evening with his rifle and lamp, saw two pairs of gleaming eyes staring from the darkness, and fired a round of ammunition, killing both animals. Upon closer examination the confused Texan found he had shot his own team of horses.

Ruckle Park Headquarters.

A barn along Beaver Point Road was once used by its owner as a hideout from special constables investigating a murder in 1907. The farmer, a man named Williams, was hosting a party which became wildly out of control as the booze was imbibed. No longer able to control his rowdy houseguests, Williams loudly announced he was retiring for the evening and would shoot anyone who attempted to follow him up the ladder to the loft.

The threat was ignored by one particularly jovial souse who ascended the ladder to be greeted by a spray of buckshot. Both the man and party immediately expired. The next day a sad and sober Williams was found hiding in his barn; after a trial and conviction, he was sentenced to life imprisonment.

Transportation

B.C. ferries to Saltspring from the lower mainland and Vancouver Island run several times a day throughout the year. With daily commuters, a growing population, and increasing tourists, ferry service to Saltspring is well used. Terminals may become crowded in summer, but waits are rarely intolerable.

Long Harbour is the terminal for sailings from the mainland at Tsawwassen and reservations for vehicles may be required (check with B.C. Ferry Corporation). Ferries from outer Gulf Islands also arrive at Long Harbour. Vesuvius Bay is the terminal for sailings from Crofton, on Vancouver Island 75 kilometres north of Victoria. Ships from Swartz Bay arrive on Saltspring at Fulford Harbour. In recent years there has been talk, to the chagrin of islanders, of moving the Fulford terminal to Isabella Point, at the southwest entrance to Fulford Harbour.

Check telephone directories (Saltspring Island has its own) or the Travel Infocentre in Ganges for information about airlines and water taxis serving the island. The Travel Infocentre or local businesses can also provide information on buses, taxis, and car and bicycle rentals.

Emergencies and Information

In an emergency on Saltspring Island get to a phone and dial 911. Lady Minto Hospital and an RCMP detachment are located in Ganges.

A Travel Infocentre is usually in operation on Saltspring. Local stores, resorts and businesses are generally good sources for island information. The weekly *Gulf Islands Driftwood*, described in Chapter 1, is published in Ganges and provides excellent news coverage of Saltspring, along with a touch of tasteful gossip.

Camping and Accommodation

Ruckle Provincial Park, totalling more than 480 hectares, is at the end of Beaver Point Road, 10 kilometres from the Fulford ferry terminal. A few motorhome campers can set up in wooded parking areas, but the best camping is on the waterfront. It has about 40 walk-in campsites and gear must be packed a couple of hundred metres from a parking lot. It's

Officer and ice cream.

ideal for hikers and cyclists. Tents can be pitched in small clusters of trees and in open fields overlooking Swanson and Satellite channels.

B.C. ferries running in and out of Swartz Bay pass so close to Beaver Point that campers often feel vibrations from the ships' engines rumbling the ground. Illuminated ships are particularly fascinating to watch as they cruise by in the night. This may well be the Gulf Islands' most attractive campsite.

Mouat Provincial Park, in Ganges, is a 23-hectare campground with 15 sites. It is generally used by recreation vehicles and campers who want to be near the amenities of town. It seems almost out of place — a quiet, forested oasis in the midst of the bustle and activity of downtown Ganges.

Some resorts on Saltspring have campgrounds with showers and RV hookups.

Being such a large, busy and accessible island, Saltspring has a wide range of accommodations, from lodges and inns, to cottage resorts, motels, hotels, and bed-and-breakfast outlets. Many of the places to stay on Saltspring are published in Tourism B.C.'s annual *Accommodations* booklet, described in Chapter 1. Information on accommodation may also be available from telephone directories, local tourist information centres, Travel Infocentres throughout B.C., and from brochure racks on B.C. ferries. It's wise to book well ahead for a holiday on Saltspring.

Shopping and Services

Stores, pubs, restaurants and other commercial establishments are

Fulford public wharf.

located around Saltspring in population centres such as Fulford Harbour, Fernwood or Vesuvius Bay. The village of Ganges has all the amenities required by the island's burgeoning population. Financial institutions, supermarkets, hardware stores, bicycle shops, government agents, service stations, restaurants, pubs, marinas, post offices, laundromats, public showers, liquor outlets, information centres, real estate offices, shoe repair shops, pharmacies, bookstores, and more are available to Saltspring Islanders.

Newcomers are often taken aback by the fuss and bustle on the streets of downtown Ganges: it's rarely quiet, with shoppers pouring in and out of malls and specialty shops, families strolling along the seawalk in Centennial Park, children swinging in the adventure playground, condominium owners peering from their balconies over the waters of Ganges Harbour, and cyclists, motorists and pedestrians trying to avoid one another on the busy roads. Ganges belies the belief that the Gulf Islands are just a sleepy backwater for society dropouts.

Saltspring is well known for its abundance of writers, artists and craftsmen. Galleries, studios and shops throughout the island display and sell locally produced work.

Recreation and Events

Golfers, bowlers and tennis players can pursue their sports on Saltspring. There are ample facilities for boaters and sailors, and local sources can provide detail on canoe, kayak and boat rentals, fishing, diving and cruising charters, bicycle rentals and tours, guided nature hikes and cruises, horseback trips and other outdoor activities.

The island also hosts several major events, including open markets, craft fairs, art shows, barbecues, sheep dog trials and more.

Saltspring Island Hiking — Different Hikes for Different Types

Beaver Point Park

Beaver Point Provincial Park is often confused with Ruckle Park, a much larger public area at the end of Beaver Point Road. En route to Ruckle Park you will pass the Beaver Point Community Hall and an old, one-room school on the left side of the road. This is Beaver Point Park, a 16-hectare forest infrequently visited by hikers.

You can walk through this forest under sizeable cedars, Douglas firs, alders and maples. Spanish moss dangles from some trees and lush green mosses cover the deadfalls. Some standing snags have been mercilessly attacked by woodpeckers. The higher parts of the park are embellished by arbutus and Garry oak.

Ruckle Provincial Park

Ruckle Provincial Park, encompassing more than 480 hectares, seven kilometres of shoreline and eight coves, is undoubtedly the easiest hiking ground on Saltspring. Most of the land is at sea level and the few hills

Hiking a Saltspring backroad.

are low and rolling, offering little difficulty for elderly or sedentary hikers. Because of the great expanse of open, grassy meadow along the seashore, there has been little need to build a trail system. There are, however, a few trails or roads on the wooded points and in the forests up from the shore.

The land was owned by the Ruckle family and part of the park is still operated as a farm. The rustic, meticulously maintained buildings provide a pleasant setting for a stroll along a country road. Backpackers and cyclists who arrive on the island as foot passengers aboard the ferries often hike or cycle the 10 kilometres from Fulford Harbour to Beaver Point.

In the 1920s Beaver Point was used by rumrunners as a stash for liquor smuggled across the Canada-United States border. A member of the Ruckle family, Alfred Ruckle, was once wandering along the shore when his dog sniffed out a trail in the woods and stumbled upon several cases of whisky. Alfred Ruckle, not a greedy man, took one bottle. He returned the next day to inspect the cache and all of the liquor was gone.

Peter Arnell Park

This local park offers an alternative to the rugged trails of Mount Maxwell Park or Saltspring's south end. Although Douglas fir and cedar are plentiful, much of the forest is alder and maple: the deciduous prominence gives the woods a somewhat brighter atmosphere than that found in a typical evergreen forest.

Peter Arnell Park is on Stewart Road, about two kilometres from the intersection of Stewart and Beaver Point roads. From the Ganges side,

Ruckle Park in winter.

71

Stewart Road is accessible via Beddis and Cusheon Lake roads. The park appears at a sharp bend on Stewart Road. In the woods above the inside of the bend is a monument to Peter Arnell, a young surveyor who was accidentally killed while working on Galiano Island.

On the opposite side of the road from the monument, trails through the woods are marked. This trail network is slated for improvement during the 1990s, extending the trails through the park and beyond to provide access for hikers to Cusheon Beach, a shallow, clam-digging beach with views across Captain Passage to Prevost Island and the Channel Islands. There's sea-run cutthroat fishing here off the mouth of Cusheon Creek.

Mount Maxwell Provincial Park

There are an estimated seven kilometres of hiking trails in Mount Maxwell Provincial Park, some leading down steep slopes and ridges through stately evergreen forests, others ending on high bluffs overlooking Vancouver Island and the waters which separate it from Saltspring. The park, totalling 197 hectares, is most easily reached by Cranberry Road, which runs off Fulford-Ganges Road near the top of Ganges Hill. Although the park road is a public highway, it is not plowed during winter.

The park adjoins a 64-hectare ecological reserve that begins about 1.5 kilometres from the summit and covers the slopes to the northwest side of Baynes Peak. The reserve was established in 1972 to preserve an

On Musgrave Road.

72

undisturbed stand of Garry oak, B.C.'s only native species of oak tree. From Baynes Peak, at 595 metres, are Saltspring's best views of Burgoyne Bay, the Fulford Valley and Sansum Narrows.

As Mount Maxwell is not a high-use park, the trails are not marked and receive little maintenance. Generally, the trails begin near the parking lot and picnic tables at the end of the park road and run in loops parallel to the road. There is a one-kilometre trail which follows the ocean view from the parking lot to a sharp bend in the road. If you take the trail as far as the road, you can walk back toward the parking lot for a short distance, then pick up a trail on the left side of the road. That trail leads through the woods to the parking lot. Because of the low maintenance on the trails a map and compass are advisable, but if you keep a mental record of landmarks, it is usually no problem to return to the road.

The Mountains of Saltspring's Rugged South End

Saltspring's mountainous south end is among the finest hiking country in the Gulf Islands. From the little-used road to Mount Tuam, Bruce Peak or Musgrave Landing, there are striking views over Satellite Channel to Vancouver Island, the southern Gulf Islands and the northern San Juan Islands in Washington State. This entire area is accessible by Musgrave Road, a lumpy dirt road that runs from sea level at Fulford Harbour, on the northeast side of the mountains, to sea level at Musgrave Landing, on

Little Lake.

the southwest side. Mid-point on Musgrave Road, a 14.4-kilometre public highway, is also the highest point, where it climbs nearly 600 metres between Bruce Peak and Hope Hill.

The road begins near the head of Fulford Harbour on Fulford-Ganges Road and forks at a small lake 6.4 kilometres up the mountain. This lake may dry during hot summers. As many as a dozen bald eagles might be perched on the limbs of dead snags rising from the lake. If you want pictures, your camera and telephoto lens should be readied before getting out of the car. Approach the eagles as quietly and slowly as possible.

You can drive all the way to Bruce Peak, Mount Tuam or Musgrave Landing, but the road becomes progressively worse and hiking is easier on both the car and the nerves. It is best to find somewhere to park off the road by the lake or junction and begin any of the three hikes here.

Bruce Peak

The incredible, panoramic view from Bruce Peak, 1.6 kilometres from the junction by the lake, rivals any other found in the Gulf Islands. The peak, at 698 metres, is the highest point in the islands. On a clear day you can look east across Pender and Saturna islands and see the sun glistening off the wintry summit of Washington State's Mount Baker, more than 120 kilometres away. If Georgia Strait is calm, B.C. ferries running in and out of Tsawwassen, on the B.C. mainland, can be seen through binoculars or a telescope directly across from Active Pass. Ferries and boats are visible in Fulford Harbour and in the channels near Russell, Portland and Moresby islands to the southeast.

On the southwest side of the peak you can look directly down at Separation Point, separating Cowichan Bay from Sansum Narrows. The view from this side looks over the Sooke Hills and watershed, the source of water for Greater Victoria.

There are a forestry lookout and B.C. Telephone Company microwave repeater station at the top, which should be left undisturbed.

Fortune seekers who drilled for diamonds on this mountain discovered traces of gold and a fine grade of iron. The iron deposits were not substantial enough to mine but a significant amount of quartz and rhodonite was taken from Bruce Peak.

Mount Tuam

It is believed "Old Bald Face," as it was known by the local natives, derives its name from the Indian word *chu'an*, meaning "facing the sun." Tuam's barren 630-metre peak rises over Satellite Channel, a monumental reminder to Saanich Peninsula residents that the peace of the Gulf Islands is fewer than two kilometres away.

The top of the mountain is four kilometres from the Bruce Peak fork. About 1.8 kilometres from the fork there is another junction, where the road goes right to Musgrave Landing; go straight ahead to Mount Tuam. As you approach the summit the forest becomes sparse, giving way to open areas of rock and pasture. Near the top there is a deteriorating Ministry of Transport gate to stop people from driving to the installations at the peak. The equipment provides important navigational assistance to aircraft and marine broadcasts for recreational boaters. Tampering with it could cause a serious accident.

Inside the gate you can look directly to the west across Separation Point and Mount Tzuhalem into Cowichan and Genoa bays. To the south you can see down Saanich Inlet, beyond Senanus Island and Brentwood Bay, to the beginning of Finlayson Arm, the southernmost reach of the inlet. Closer to you, on the northwest side of Saanich Peninsula, you will see Deep Cove, the federal Institute of Ocean Sciences at Patricia Bay, and Victoria International Airport.

The views over the peninsula and nearby islands are awesome. On the east side you will see the long, sandy outline of Sidney Spit Marine Park and the heavily wooded islands around it. On the same side of the peninsula you will see Canoe Cove, Swartz Bay and several islands clustered around the B.C. ferry terminal.

The peak and south slopes are moist and green in spring when Easter lilies, pink shooting stars, trilliums and other wildflowers bloom, but summer sun turns the pastures dry and brown, giving Mount Tuam a look which remotely resembles that of the mountains around B.C.'s Okanagan Valley.

There is a 251-hectare ecological reserve on Mount Tuam, which runs along Saltspring's southern shoreline in two places. Ecological reserves are created in B.C. to preserve natural features which are unique or representative of the area. They are often used for education or research and remain open to the public on the firm understanding that nothing will be touched. The ecological reserve on Mount Tuam preserves a forest of Douglas fir, broad-leafed maple, western red cedar, arbutus and red alder.

Musgrave Landing

The distinctive aroma of the sea and mild ocean breezes become increasingly conspicuous as you near the end of a 6.4-kilometre trek to Musgrave Landing. Majestic stands of Douglas fir, interspersed with smooth and twisted arbutus, are slowly replacedby giant cedars, alders and eventually dogwoods with their creamy white spring flowers.

Musgrave Landing, with public and private wharves, is slightly less than seven kilometres from the Mount Tuam-Bruce Peak fork near the little lake. The bumpy track runs down to the right, off the road to Mount Tuam, just under two kilometres from the lake. It is a public highway, which gradually descends to the sea at Musgrave Landing, then carries on to subdivisions along the shores of Sansum Narrows. The descent is not steep but it is steady, something to keep in mind for the return trip. It can be hiked one way in about an hour and a half.

About a kilometre from Musgrave Landing you will hear a creek which flows through a deep ravine parallel to the road. Shortly after the creek disappears you will reach a fork in the road. Musgrave Landing is five minutes straight ahead, but a left turn takes you to a government greenbelt area with a beach facing a large rock, known locally as Musgrave Island.

The greenbelt area, totalling 35 hectares, was purchased in 1974 for public recreational use, but camping is discouraged because no facilities are available and summer fire hazard is high. The land was formerly a farm and several sheep roam the wooded hills and open pastures. If you follow an overgrown road through the farm, you will reach a pretty creek with a waterfall. Another overgrown road leads down to a beach facing Musgrave Island, a good beach for clam-digging.

The long climb back to the car is not difficult, but because the ascent is steady, it can be tiring and a bit hard on hikers without proper boots. A bottle of water and some insect repellent are worth carrying on warm days.

SALTSPRING'S MOUNTAINOUS SOUTH END

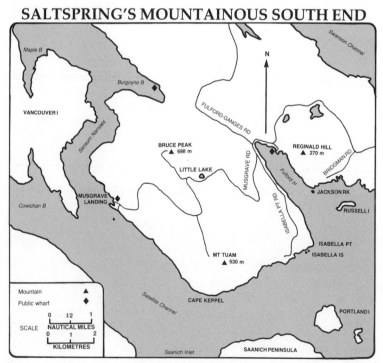

Canoeing and Small Boating —
For Families and Intrepid Voyageurs

Fulford Harbour to Musgrave Landing

Distance: 18 nautical miles return. *Launching:* Drummond Park on Fulford Harbour or Fulford government dock.

Musgrave Landing is a tiny cove tucked behind Musgrave Point at the foot of Saltspring's steep southwest slopes. It is used by yachtsmen as a refuge from brisk summer winds which blow up Satellite Channel from the southeast.

There are several good camping beaches between Musgrave Landing and Cape Keppel, at the foot of Mount Tuam, but private property should be respected.

The journey from Fulford to Musgrave takes three or four hours by manually powered boat, depending on the tides, and during summer it is best started in late afternoon to take advantage of the evening calm and fiery sunset as you travel along the southwest shore of Saltspring. Boat wash from traffic in Satellite Channel is generally insignificant but caution should be exercised around Isabella Point and Islets near the beginning of the voyage. Ferries from Swartz Bay and Fulford Harbour create large swells that can be dangerous to small boats.

The beautiful gravel beaches near Isabella Islets are as interesting as this area's history. Isabella Point was first settled by Kanakas, from

Isabella Point.

77

Hawaii, who were known for their unique method of curing locally grown tobacco and their boisterous, seemingly endless luaus. A group of 18 Hawaiians originally took up residence on Isabella Point and Portland Island, now a provincial marine park on the other side of Satellite Channel.

When they were struck by the urge to celebrate, canoes would be loaded with food and their own befuddling home brew. The intemperance and musical merriment would begin on Portland Island and carry on from house to house until the last morsel was devoured and all the swill was swallowed. It was not uncommon for these exhaustive luaus to run into several days, even weeks.

As you approach Cape Keppel, marked by a triangular white fisheries boundary sign at the foot of Mount Tuam, a long, gravel beach rounds the cape and continues a good distance along the southwest side of the island toward Musgrave Landing. This is a good area for sea lion sightings and salmon fishing. It never hurts to troll a lightly weighted spoon or bucktail for the entire journey, particularly when mature cohoes are running in late summer and fall.

Near Cape Keppel you will pass through a marine ecological reserve, totalling 339 hectares. It covers the bottom of Satellite Channel between the south shore of Mount Tuam and Moses Point, on Saanich Peninsula. The plant and animal life found on the sea floor here is representative of southern Gulf Island marine life. The reserve is often used for study by biologists from the University of Victoria and it is illegal for recreational scuba divers to collect specimens here.

Fulford Harbour to Jackson Rock

Distance: three nautical miles return. *Launching:* Drummond Park or Fulford government dock.

Fulford Harbour is lazy canoeing water for loafers who would rather catch a few sunrays than exercise their biceps. You can plan the day over a home-cooked breakfast at a cafe, then take on a shot of extra fuel at the local inn before launching. It is interesting to poke around the docks and pilings near the ferry terminal where you can count on finding a few out-of-the-ordinary boats tied up or moored in the bay, but stay out of the way of ferries moving in and out of the docks. Past the terminal along the northeast shore are two pretty coves where creeks from Stowell and Weston lakes flow to the sea.

During the last century the waters of Fulford Harbour were favourite duck-hunting grounds for Indians. When migratory waterfowl arrived at Fulford in winter, the Indians would close off the mouth of the harbour with a paddle-to-paddle line of canoes. The bay, at that time skirted by dense forests, would be deathly silent as the canoes glided into the harbour, blocking off all escape routes for the unsuspecting quarry. At a given signal the sound of whistling arrows and panic-stricken birds would shatter the silence. When the slaughter was over and morbid quiet restored, the women would fill pick-up canoes with the dead and dying victims of the raid.

You can hug the shoreline in a small boat and pull out on a number of beaches if a wind comes up. Wash from the ferries is not usually bothersome by the time it reaches the shore, but it is wise to keep an eye on it. On the way to Jackson Rock you will pass Reginald Hill, recently subdivided for residential development, but once the scene of frequent bloodshed from Indian warfare.

The Indians of the Gulf Islands were constantly on the lookout for unwelcome arrivals of Haida and Bella Bella natives from the north. In order to protect their camps at Fulford, scouts were posted at the top of Reginald Hill and boulders were strategically mounted on ridges above the shore. When attackers approached from the sea, the women and children were relegated to the safety of the forest while the men greeted the raiders with flying arrows and bouncing boulders.

On the south side of Reginald Hill there is an Indian reserve covering the entire point at the end of Fulford Harbour. Off the point is Jackson Rock, an islet with unusually bright shell beaches and clear shallow waters. Low tide is the best time to visit Jackson Rock, as much of it is submerged at high tide.

People occasionally camp on the Indian reserve across from the rock, but it should be remembered that the land is privately owned. The reserve's last permanent inhabitant was Indian Charlie, a noted fisherman who mysteriously vanished shortly before becoming a Great Chief. Indian Charlie

Jackson Rock.

was three times a widower. Each time a wife died he purchased a new one from the nearby Cowichan band for $20. It is assumed that Indian Charlie and his last wife were murdered and robbed only a few days before holding a potlatch to be attended by neighbouring Great Chiefs. Their canoe was found on Portland Island after their inexplicable disappearance.

Jackson Rock can also be reached in a small boat from a beach that faces Russell Island, a privately owned island off the southeast end of Saltspring. To find the beach, located at the end of a B.C. Department of Highways access, drive along Beaver Point Road to Bridgman Road, turn onto Menhinick Drive at the end of Bridgman and follow the road a short distance from the turn.

Chain Islands in Ganges Harbour

Distance: four nautical miles. *Launching:* beach at the end of Churchill Road or Ganges government dock.

As you drive along Fulford-Ganges Road, high above the southwest side of Ganges Harbour, you will catch tantalizing glimpses of the Chain Islands. A miniature archipelago on the harbour's northeast side, the islands and drying reefs among them are an undeclinable invitation to small boaters. They are especially appealing to families or inexperienced canoeists because they stretch the full length of the harbour, yet they are fairly protected from all but southeasterly winds. The crossings from island to island are short, and the safety of shore is never more than a few strokes away.

A leisurely three-hour cruise in a circle around the group can be done at any time when winds are light. Mink are commonly seen scurrying over the rocks at low tide, and if you keep an eye astern, you might find you are being tailed by a curious harbour seal or riber otter. Bald eagles keep a constant watch from the treetops, while seabirds — gulls, cormorants, diving ducks and black oystercatchers — sedulously scour the intertidal zone for seashore delicacies.

The Chain Islands are privately owned and there are houses on most. At the northwest end of Third Sister, the largest of the Three Sister Islands, there is a small shell beach, a good place for a rest or afternoon picnic. Deadman Island, between Goat Island and the Three Sisters, is so named for its use in the 1800s as an Indian burial ground.

It was near this island, in the summer of 1860, that nine Bella Bella Indians met an untimely death at the hands of about 50 bloodthirsty Cowichans. The Bella Bellas, with three women, two boys and a white man, arrived in Ganges Harbour, where they dropped off their white passenger and accepted an invitation from the Cowichans to rest on the shore.

The Cowichans immediately opened fire on the Bella Bella Indians, massacring eight of the men and letting one escape critically wounded. The women and children were taken as slaves.

The savage incident did not go unrevenged. A few days after the bloodshed, two Cowichan Indians were fishing from a canoe in Ganges Harbour. Two white men were fishing nearby. A fleet of canoes paddled by Fort Rupert Indians, friends of the Bella Bellas, appeared around a point and headed directly for the two Cowichans. The Cowichans, unaware of the earlier slaughter, abandoned their craft and jumped aboard the boat occupied by the white men. The Fort Ruperts swarmed the Cowichans, plunged knives into their half-naked bodies and decapitated both victims. Keeping the heads, the attackers dumped the headless bodies in the sea and departed, leaving the horrified white fishermen unharmed. This was one of the last clashes between warring Indians in the Gulf Islands.

Canoeing the Chain Islands.

Long Harbour

Distance: four nautical miles. *Launching:* beach at the end of Quebec Drive.

Scott Point, on the southwest side of Long Harbour, is a favourite roost for bald eagles. As many as two dozen of these stately raptors can be seen perched boldly atop the evergreens near the tip of the point. They are fairly easy to spot, as they nearly always sit at the top, or within a few boughs of the top, of the tree. Eagles are easily spooked, so photographers should have their cameras and telephotos ready for shooting at the outset of the journey. If you keep an itchy finger on the shutter until the last minute, you might be lucky enough to snap an adult eagle showing off a full wingspan of two metres.

Although the distance from the launching point at the end of Quebec Drive to the mouth of the harbour is only two nautical miles, enough time should be set aside for a journey up one side and down the other, about two hours. Southeasters occasionally puff into the harbour but Prevost Island, directly across from Nose Point, acts as a partial barrier to unwelcome winds.

Nose Point, about 250 metres across the harbour mouth from Scott Point, forms the northern side of Long Harbour. There are a group of islets and a couple of coves near the end of Nose Point, an intriguing place to putter. A beach near the islets at Nose Point is a good picnic spot with warm summer swimming. If you continue over the mud flats at the head of the harbour when the tide is high you will add another two nautical miles to the voyage.

Ganges Harbour, with enough boating water for a weekend of exploration, can be reached by portaging across Scott Point Drive immediately southeast of the B.C. ferry terminal. A light boat can be hauled up a three-metre embankment to level ground. On the opposite side of the road is another steep but short trail leading down to Welbury Bay, which is adjacent to Ganges Harbour.

Walker Hook

Distance: three nautical miles. *Launching:* beach at the end of the road opposite the intersection of Walker's Hook Road and Fort Street.

A quick paddle or row around Walker Hook is a nice break from an afternoon of driving or a good time filler while you are waiting for a ferry from Long Harbour. From the launching place you can go around the point and look across Trincomali Channel to Galiano Island. To the northeast you will see the entrance to Montague Harbour, location of one of the most frequently visited marine parks in the Gulf Islands. Less than half a nautical mile from the point is the crook of the hook, which is private land. From here there is a clear view along the northeast side of Saltspring to the entrance to Captain Passage off Nose Point.

Several miles can be added to a tour of Walker Hook by travelling toward the north end of Saltspring and around Southey Point. The shore between Walker Hook and the north end of Saltspring is rock and sand, with several beaches to explore. Though tides and winds in Trincomali Channel often create rough seas, the paddle toward Southey Point is a pleasant sightseeing journey on a warm summer or autumn day.

There's a government wharf and general store at Fernwood, where supplies can be purchased and letters posted. For a break from the chilly waters of Trincomali Channel, St. Mary Lake is a two-kilometre walk from Fernwood via North Beach and North End roads. There's fairly good cod fishing off Victoria Rock near Fernwood Point.

Southey Point, Saltspring's most northerly tip, is a populated area with several cottages and permanent homes. It's a pretty area with a number of bays and coves, beaches and arbutus-covered shores. Many canoeists use it as a launching point for journeys to places on both sides of Saltspring.

Tent Island was once leased from the Indians of Kuper Island for use as a provincial park, but the park no longer exists and the island remains as private Indian land. The shorelines of Kuper and Tent islands are similar to those of Saltspring's northeast side, and while it is against the law to land on the beaches, they are intriguing spots to explore from a boat.

Much of the sea off the north end of Saltspring is warm for summer swimming.

Southey Point to Idol Island

Distance: three nautical miles. *Launching:* at the end of Southey Point Road or Arbutus Road.

Half a nautical mile south of Stone Cutters Bay is an inconspicuous runt of an island that serves no useful purpose other than of mere existence. Once used as an Indian burial ground, Idol Island is now a park reserve that is generally ignored by the boating public. Provincial parks officials have no plans for the island and anyone is welcome to camp on it.

To a passing boater, Idol Island appears as a rocky lump rising seven metres out of the sea with a few scrubby trees clumped on the top. The view is not great, the only beach is minuscule, and the wildlife is scarce — perhaps the odd crow or seagull. The starkness of this dwarfish islet is undoubtedly its most saleable feature: nobody goes there.

A pleasant trip past a populated shoreline from Southey Point gets you to Idol Island in about an hour. Dozens of cozy cottages are scattered along the route, many artistically embellished with driftwood sculptures and miscellaneous nautical paraphernalia from nearby beaches. The island is far enough from shore to provide reasonable seclusion and one tent, possible two, could be squeezed onto a tiny beach on the southwest side.

There is a certain scenic similarity to the different bays near Southey Point, which can be confusing to visitors unfamiliar with the area. If the tide is low when you launch your boat, for example, the launching point could look quite different if you return at high tide. Take a good look at the landmarks before embarking to avoid difficulty finding your car on the way back. Your car probably will not be visible from the water, so a clear mental picture of the nearby features will help you locate it.

Southey Point to the Secretary Islands

Distance: ten nautical miles. *Launching:* at the end of Southey Point Road.

The Secretary Islands, north of Southey Point, provide one of the finest overnight small-boating trips in the Gulf Islands and can be part of a much longer expedition which could take a week or more. Though this group has few beaches, there are a couple of good campsites and numerous bays and reefs to explore, many inaccessible to larger vessels.

SOUTHEY POINT AREA

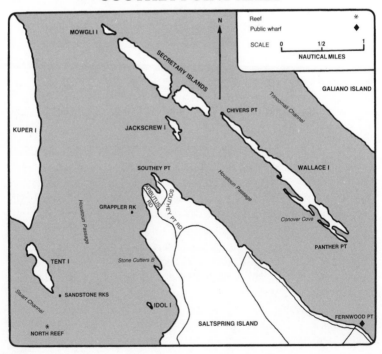

The crossing from Southey Point to Jackscrew Island is only half a nautical mile and it is another half-mile to the most southerly of the two Secretary Islands. This chain, which includes the Secretary Islands, and Mowgli and Wallace islands, is also accessible by small boat from Retreat Cove on Galiano Island, but that crossing is nearly one and a half miles.

All of these islands are privately owned but the two Secretary Islands are uninhabited. Much of the shoreline around this group is strewn with reefs and avoided by some yachtsmen who would rather move on to more easily navigable waters than risk piling up on an unseen reef. However, the reefs provide additional shelter for small boats as well as an interesting system of shallow channels that can be toured without the worry of being swamped by inconsiderate power boaters.

The owners of Wallace Island discourage camping and there are few suitable campsites in the whole group. There is, however, a good beach on the southwest side of the lower Secretary Island, across from Jackscrew Island, and a few others along the same shoreline toward Mowgli Island.

From the tip of the upper Secretary Island, Hall and Reid islands can be circumnavigated and some boaters like to slip through the gap between Thetis and Kuper islands. From Telegraph Harbour there is a pleasant journey down the side of Kuper to Tent Island.

Arbutus Beach to Vesuvius Bay

Distance: eight nautical miles return. *Launching:* Arbutus Beach at the end of Collins Road off Rainbow Road.

Canoeing the Secretary Islands.

85

Arbutus Beach, also known as Cranberry Outlet, is a quarter-mile north of Erskine Point on the shores of Stuart Channel. It is a good launching point for small boats and trailer boats for the trip to Vesuvius and Booth bays.

A short, overgrown road from the south side of Maxwell Creek leads to Erskine Point for partial views down Sansum Narrows. The narrows begin at Erskine Point but because of the increase in tidal velocity from the point down, canoeists and small boaters should watch their water if venturing south of the point. Like Musgrave Landing, Arbutus Beach is a good viewpoint for sunsets over Vancouver Island.

A one-mile cruise along the shore north of Arbutus Beach takes you to the entrance to Booth Inlet. The intertidal mudflats in the inlet offer an enchanting type of scenery that is not to be found anywhere else on Saltspring, except possibly at the head of Long Harbour. As you navigate the narrow gap between the inlet and Booth Bay, the atmosphere changes abruptly from that of open water to one of complacency and confinement. The fragrance of the ocean becomes more profound; there is a pond-like stillness, periodically broken by the chatter of fluttering kingfishers.

A casual drift up the inlet at high tide ends at a bridge on Booth Canal Road, a useable launching point for shallow-draught boats. Plans to dredge a canal between Booth Inlet and Ganges Harbour have been bandied about in the past, but nothing has ever come of them. You are not likely to make it as far as the bridge at low water, when some parts of the inlet are so shallow that you occasionally hear the sound of mucky sand gently scraping the hull. Once through the mouth of the inlet, the depth is usually sufficient for outboard motors.

Booth Inlet.

A run along the north shore of Booth Bay to Vesuvius Bay is just over one nautical mile. Small boats can also be launched at a public wharf next to the Vesuvius ferry terminal, or from a beach with access from Langley Street off Vesuvius Bay Road.

St. Mary Lake

Distance: four miles, total shoreline. *Launching:* at the side of North End Road.

Canoeing St. Mary Lake.

87

St. Mary Lake, with a total water surface of 200 hectares, is the largest body of fresh water in the Gulf Islands. The number of resorts located on the shores of St. Mary Lake is clear evidence of its popularity as a vacation spot. It is unfortunate that government authorities have failed so miserably in setting aside lakefront land for public use here.

A cruise around the entire shoreline is a pleasant afternoon trip, and if the sun gets too hot there are a number of rocky spots on the west side to stop for a dip. There is also a cluster of rocks about 300 metres in front of the launching spot on North End Road where you can pull out your boat and stop for a rest or swim. There are houses and resorts in the two main bays at the north end of the lake but most of the western side is sparsely populated.

The lake lies in a low valley with wooded hillsides rising to 290 metres on the west. Trincomali Heights, a growing residential district, rises to 210 metres on the east.

Cusheon Lake

Distance: two miles, total shoreline. *Launching:* off Cusheon Lake Road; no motorboats.

A family of river otters can frequently be seen splashing around the marshes and lily pads at the edge of Cusheon Lake. They seem to be especially fond of the narrow arm at the southeast end where they can hide under cover of overhanging branches. Like the eagles of Scott Point, the otters are leery of intruders, so cameras and telephotos should be prepared at the outset of the trip.

Cusheon Creek drains from the southeast end into Captain Passage at the mouth of Ganges Harbour, and a creek running from Roberts and Blackburn Lakes feeds Cusheon from the northwest.

When You Arrive by Private Boat

Although Saltspring is at the westernmost edge of the southern Gulf Islands, it actually lies at the centre of British Columbia's most significant cruising area. It almost touches the shores of Vancouver Island on the west; Saanich Inlet and Peninsula are less than two miles to the south, and numerous islands and islets surround Saltspring on the east and north sides.

There are several interesting anchorages around Saltspring, and while this section offers some information about those places, it is suggested that boaters read other parts of the book, such as sections on hiking, fishing, canoeing and small boating, and services for additional information.

The areas listed here would be encountered in this order if you circumnavigated Saltspring in a counter-clockwise direction from Ganges.

Ganges Harbour

Ganges, named after what was the fastest sailing ship in the Royal Navy during the mid-1800s, is the Gulf Islands' major commercial centre. There are numerous anchorages protected from all but southeast winds and a government wharf, sheltered by a breakwater, at the head of the harbour. There is plenty of moorage space but you may have to tie alongside another boat. Another government wharf on the opposite side of Grace Peninsula is not as well protected.

Fuel and boat repairs are available and all the facilities of the town are within walking distance. There are many restaurants, a pub and lounge and tennis courts in town, and a golf course about two kilometres from the government wharf. Any groceries or supplies you may need can be purchased in Ganges, and a post office is behind the bank across from the waterfront. Lady Minto Gulf Islands Hospital and an RCMP detachment are located here.

Long Harbour

Long Harbour, as the name implies, is a long, narrow inlet used as a terminus for ferries from Tsawwassen. It is sheltered from all but southeast winds and is particularly attractive near the head of the harbour. The mudflats here are fun to explore by dinghy when there is ample water. Scott Point Road, which begins near the ferry terminal, is a pleasant walk for a look at some interesting cottage and house designs. Bald eagles roost in the trees above the inlet.

Near the entrance to the harbour is Prevost Island, one of the largest undeveloped Gulf Islands, with at least seven major bays and inlets. The island is private property but the bays offer good anchorages and protection from most winds.

Walker Hook and Fernwood

Walker Hook, on the northern side of Saltspring, is fairly exposed and the bay on the eastern side dries at low tide. It does provide some temporary refuge from southeast winds and is a nice lunch stop for boaters travelling in Trincomali Channel.

There is no shelter at Fernwood, but the government dock has space for two or three boats. North Beach Road, at the head of the wharf, makes a nice stroll, and St. Mary Lake is a two-kilometre walk from Fernwood.

Southey Point

The shoreline between Fernwood and Southey Point forms the southern side of Houstoun Passage. Across the passage, Wallace Island and the Secretary Islands, described in the section on canoeing and small boating in this chapter, provide some good anchorages.

There are good moorages in Southey and Stone Cutters bays, protected from all but northwest winds, but the shoreline is covered by private homes.

Vesuvius Bay

There is a government wharf at Vesuvius, conveniently located a few steps from a store, a motel, a restaurant and a neighbourhood pub. A stroll among the farms and forests along Sunset Drive is a good way to stretch your legs; for energetic boaters, there are tennis courts at Portlock Park, slightly more than three kilometres from the wharf.

On the northwest side of Vesuvius there are anchorages in tiny coves behind Dock and Parminter points. Booth Bay and Inlet, southeast of Vesuvius, offer protection from southeasters.

Burgoyne Bay

Burgoyne Bay, at the foot of Mount Maxwell, forms the western end of the Fulford Valley. It is exposed to winds from the southeast and northwest but offers good temporary anchorage in the shallows near the head of the bay, where there is good summer swimming, a sandy beach and fair crab fishing. The oysters, however, are under a private lease.

A small government wharf is located near a booming ground. Maple Bay and Birds Eye Cove, on Vancouver Island, are across Sansum Narrows from Burgoyne Bay. Nearly all boating necessities, including marinas, a government wharf, and a well-known pub with floats, are available in Maple Bay.

Musgrave Landing

The narrowest part of Sansum Narrows is between Bold Bluff, at the southwest entrance to Burgoyne Bay, and Sansum Point on Vancouver Island. This area is known for both its excellent salmon fishing and its unparalleled beauty. Many Gulf Island boaters consider Sansum Narrows, with peaks rising to 233 metres on Vancouver Island and more than 620 metres on Saltspring, one of the most scenic waterways in the islands. The distance across the channel at Bold Bluff is less than three-tenths of a mile and it rarely widens to more than half a mile as it curves in an S-bend toward Satellite Channel.

Musgrave Landing is a comfortable cove with government and private docks. It is protected from most winds and there is room for a few boats to anchor, but it is often badly shaken by wash from passing boats. There is also some anchorage in two little bays northwest of Musgrave Landing.

This nook is a popular spot among Saanich Peninsula boaters who like to get away for day-trips during winter months. There are many old logging roads near the wharf as well as an abandoned farm, which now

Musgrave Landing.

is publicly owned. The Musgrave area is described in greater detail in the section on hiking Saltspring's rugged south end.

Although there are a few homes in the Musgrave area, it is basically a wilderness region with no facilities. Cowichan and Genoa bays are a short cruise around Separation Point from Musgrave Landing and supplies can be purchased there.

Fulford Harbour

There are no good anchorages between Musgrave Landing and Fulford Harbour, with the exception of temporary holding spots near Isabella Point and Islets. Deep Cove, tucked around the northern tip of Saanich Peninsula on the western side, offers reasonably good shelter and is two miles from Cape Keppel at the southern end of Saltspring. Wain Rock, at the entrance to Deep Cove, is one of the better Saanich Inlet fishing spots.

Fulford Harbour is exposed to the southeast but is a good anchorage on calm days. There are government wharves on either side of the ferry docks. Fulford is a busy little community, the second-largest on Saltspring, with the terminal for B.C. ferries from Swartz Bay, a restaurant and store, a pub, private marina, community hall and churches.

There is easily enough to do at Fulford to keep a boating family occupied for two or three days. There is a children's park near the head of the bay, as well as beautiful beaches along Isabella Point Road, and good cutthroat trout fishing off the mouth of Fulford Creek.

Concerts and other productions featuring Saltspring talent are often held in the community hall. A walk up Morningside Road from the ferry terminal, toward Reginald Hill, is a relaxing way to start the day. Stowell Lake, a favourite fishing and swimming hole, is a 1.5-kilometre stroll along Beaver Point Road.

Beaver Point

The shoreline between Fulford Harbour and Beaver Point is intricate, with numerous coves and islets, but much of it is exposed to ferry wash. Some protection can be found behind Russell Island, a privately owned retreat near the mouth of Fulford Harbour.

Portland Island, a 192-hectare publicly owned island known as Princess Margaret Marine Park, is 2.5 miles from the mouth of Fulford Harbour on the south side of Satellite Channel. Once used to board race horses, Portland is now a picturesque, undeveloped island with abandoned orchards, a network of trails and several bays and beaches. One of the best anchorages is in Princess Bay, between Tortoise Islet and Hood Island. There is an eagle's nest on Hood Island.

Brackman Island, on the southwest side of Portland, offers fair temporary anchorage for boaters who want to explore a beautiful shell beach with grassy uplands, or dig clams at low tide. There are public floats in a cove behind Chads Island on the north side and a number of sheltered nooks on the east side. The east side, however, is surrounded by reefs, and people unfamiliar with the waters should be careful.

There are narrow bays between Eleanor and Beaver points on Saltspring and a few larger bays around the tip of Beaver Point toward Captain Passage. None of these bays are protected from ferry wash but they are usually sheltered enough to stop for a walk around Ruckle Park on Beaver Point.

Saltspring Island Fishing — Ocean, Lakes and Creeks

Fulford Harbour

Launching: Drummond Park or Fulford government wharf.

Cohoes start running off Isabella Point and Islets in late August and early September, a good time to try lightly weighted spoons or flashtails on the surface. Deeper fishing for springs here is not bad throughout the year and bottomfish can be taken in the channel between Saltspring and Russell islands. Buzz bombs and light spinning tackle occasionally catch springs and cohoes off the public wharf near the ferry terminal.

The shallows at the head of Fulford Harbour near Fulford Creek provide excellent sea-run cutthroat fishing from May throughout the summer to fall. Fish them with a fly or spinner on an incoming tide during periods of low light. Sea-run cutthroat, averaging one to three pounds in Fulford Harbour, fall within tidal water fishing regulations.

Ganges Harbour

Launching: Ganges Boat Basin.

Dungeness crabs are found along the southwest shore and near the head of the bay. Bottomfishing can be good around the Chain Islands and along the northeast side of the harbour, and sea-run cutthroat are occasionally taken from the shallows at the head of the bay.

Houstoun Passage

Launching: Arbutus Beach at the end of Collins Road.

Chinooks running up both sides of Saltspring can be caught off Southey Point and Tent Island. The springs here are not big as a rule, but they are plentiful at certain times between March and August. Bottomfishing is good off Grappler Rock or North Reef near Tent Island.

Sansum Narrows

Launching: Arbutus Beach or Fulford Harbour.

Tides up to three knots and a strong rip at Bold Bluff, coupled with winds funnelling between the high cliffs on both sides, make Sansum Narrows unsafe for small boats at certain times.

Bold Bluff is celebrated as one of the finest Gulf Island mooching areas, with winter chinooks running through January and February and cohoes taking bucktails in late summer and autumn. The powerful tide rip off Bold Bluff creates back eddies where baitfish circulate in the lower depths. Dozens of fishermen congregate off Bold Bluff and fish deep with drift-fishing lures or live herring and cut plugs on the ebb tide in early morning and evening. Mature cohoes, which begin to show near Bold Bluff in July, can be landed on buzz bombs, stingsildas, pirkens or deadly dicks at varying lengths.

There is good bucktailing in August and September and buzz bombing for big chinooks is as good as coho fishing in the fall. By September both chinook and coho runs are at their peak in the narrows. The fish are moving toward Cowichan River, so try the lower end near Burial Islet and Separation Point. Big northern cohoes to 20 pounds can be caught in September and October with trolled spoons, flashtails or squirts near the surface at Separation Point and Cowichan Bay. Much of Cowichan Bay is closed to sport fishing around this time of year when the salmon are migrating to the river.

Farther down this side of Saltspring toward Saanich Inlet, a run of chum salmon passes Cape Keppel in October and November. Chums are largely ignored by sport fishermen but they can offer some exciting buzz bombing. There are also some good clam beaches near Cape Keppel.

Satellite Channel

Launching: Fulford Harbour.

Cohoes running to the Cowichan and Goldstream rivers make Satellite Channel fair territory in late summer and fall. Wain Rock and Moses Point, at the mouth of Saanich Inlet, are among Satellite Channel's most productive areas. Big winter springs linger in the channel throughout the year and should be fished deep with herring strip or hootchies.

Saltspring's Five Good Fishing Lakes

Saltspring stands apart from all other Gulf Islands as the only one to be seriously considered by freshwater anglers. There are 12 lakes on Saltspring, five of them fished regularly. Rainbows to eight pounds have been taken on flies from Weston Lake and smallmouth bass fishing in St. Mary Lake is reputed to be the best in the province.

However, before you sneak off to Saltspring with your hook and worms, there are a few freshwater regulations of which you should be aware. Non-tidal-water licences are required for anglers 16 and over. They can be purchased on Saltspring from the government agent's office in Ganges and from stores which sell fishing tackle. Copies of regulations are available from the same outlets. Fishermen are encouraged to kill only what they intend to eat and carefully release any fish that is not destined for the dinner table.

St. Mary Lake

Launching: at the edge of North End Road.

Smallmouth bass in St. Mary Lake weigh in as high as eight pounds and take as long as 35 minutes to land. Tackle varies from sophisticated split-cane fly rods to bobbers, worms and string loosely attached to the angler's big toe. Bass, like vacationers, like it hot, so try offering a worm, muddler minnow fly, a green or orange flatfish or copper-coloured spoon in May or June. Bass in St. Mary Lake start to stir in mid-April, stay active until the end of June, then lie low until September and October.

There are some sizeable rainbows lurking in the depths of St. Mary Lake, and cutthroat, stocked by the provincial government, average a pound or a pound and a half. Take a look at the bugs floating on the surface or crawling on the bottom and try to find a fly to imitate them. If flies are in short supply, the old reliable worm is the next best bet. Trout fishing in St. Mary Lake is best in early spring, late summer and fall.

Cusheon Lake

Launching: at a small float off Cusheon Lake Road — canoes and cartoppers only, powerboats prohibited.

If you launch your boat at a small float off Cusheon Lake Road, you will see a point across the lake and slightly to the right. Cutthroat trout

Success at a Saltspring lake.

96

up to three pounds have been known to hang around about ten metres off the end of the point. Bait and bobbers catch them in February if the lake is not frozen. From April to June, or in September and October, you could try trolling a fuzzy, black wet fly or a carrot nymph around the bay behind the point. Trout have a tendency to move circularly in lakes, so if you do not have any luck in the bay, try a few casts against the shore along the opposite side of the lake, to the left of the launching float. If that doesn't work, move up the road to Blackburn Lake.

Blackburn Lake

Launching: at pullout beside highway — canoes and cartoppers, powerboats prohibited.

You will catch a glimpse of Blackburn Lake on the left side of Fulford-Ganges Road a couple of hundred metres before Cusheon Lake Road on the way to Ganges. Blackburn, much smaller than Cusheon, is linked to Cusheon Lake by a creek, and the same techniques used in Cusheon are usually successful in Blackburn. The trout in Blackburn are slightly smaller.

Stowell Lake

Launching: at the roadside float — canoes and cartoppers, only electric motors are permitted.

Stowell Lake, on Beaver Point Road, looks like an enormous puddle at the side of the road, but it is stocked with cutthroat trout up to three pounds. Fishing starts about three weeks after the ice melts in mid-March (if it freezes) and holds up until the middle of June. It picks up again in the fall and gradually declines until winter. Flies cast as close as possible around the shore take the most fish, but the odd cutthroat has been caught here on a big, green or frog-coloured flatfish trolled near the surface.

Weston Lake

Launching: on access road off Beaver Point Road — canoes and cartoppers, powerboats prohibited.

Weston is Saltspring's trophy trout lake, with rainbows tipping the scales to eight pounds. But the trout in Weston are old and wise; they are as elusive as they are large, and only the most diligent anglers emerge triumphant from a day's fishing on this little lake. Although rainbow and cutthroat trout are stocked here by the provincial government, they are not as plentiful as in other Saltspring lakes.

The attraction here is the challenge of landing a big fighter. Many anglers, satisfied with their ability to take a prize rainbow on a fly, release their prey in the hopes of catching it another day.

No part of the lake is usually more productive than another, and trial and error is the only way to get results. Flies, allowed to sink in the middle of the lake and then dragged along the bottom, occasionally attract bottom-feeders in December. Weston is the only Saltspring lake that provides summer-long trout fishing, beginning as early as March and tapering off in mid-November. The trout fishing is not as good in the middle of summer, but it is virtually nonexistent in the other lakes.

Saltspring Island Scuba Diving

Divers who need air before travelling to Saltspring should check with sources listed under the heading Information in this chapter. Divers coming from Swartz Bay or Sidney can get air from dive shops in Sidney.

Beaver Point

Shore dive — Ruckle Park at the end of Beaver Point Road.

Two small coves on the north side of Beaver Point are free of currents and abounding in marine life. Divers may find several species of bottomfish, starfish, large barnacles, anemones and octopi. Beaver Point is known among divers for its beautiful caverns and an archway about two metres high. The greatest variety of marine life here is found at a depth of about 12 or 15 metres.

Walker Hook

Shore or boat dive — launching at the end of a road opposite the intersection of Fort Street and Walker's Hook Road. Permission from the owner is needed to cross the land between the road and diving area.

Off the northeast tip of Walker Hook, a line of rocks runs parallel to the shore of Saltspring Island. Scallops and abalone can be found on the reefs at about 15 metres. The depth drops to about 30 metres on either side of the rocks.

North Reef

Boat dive — small boats can be launched at the end of Southey Point or Arbutus roads. Trailer boats at Ganges.

North Reef, off the south end of Tent Island, is celebrated for its clear visibility and insignificant currents. Boats can be anchored on the reef. North Reef is a favourite spot for shellfish such as mussels, abalone or scallops found at about 12 metres. The depth drops to more than 30 metres on either side of the reef.

Burgoyne Bay

Boat dive — small boats can be launched from the government wharf in Burgoyne Bay. Trailer boats at Ganges.

The attraction of this diving area, just northeast of Bold Bluff, is octopi lurking in their dens about 20 metres beneath the surface. These timid beasts, some with tentacles up to two metres long, can be seen hiding in caverns or stalking the bottom for food. There are a few Dungeness crabs in Burgoyne Bay, but most of the oysters fall within commercial leases, so leave them alone.

Similar underwater scenery is found around Octopus Point, across Sansum Narrows from Bold Bluff. The currents and tidal rip off Bold Bluff can be dangerous, so this area should be dived as close as possible to slack tide.

Russell Island

Boat dive — small boats can be launched at Fulford Harbour. Trailer boats at Ganges.

A couple of underwater caverns at a depth of about nine metres on the south side of Russell Island are worth exploring. Boats should be firmly anchored because of wash from passing ferries, but currents pose no problem.

After Saltspring, What Next?

The recreational opportunities on Saltspring Island, particularly for outdoors enthusiasts, are limitless. To cycle or drive all of the roads, hike the mountains and trails, travel the shores, comb the beaches and fish the best lakes would take several trips to the island. So plan several trips. And then remember, there are still the Penders, Galiano, Mayne and Saturna.

The Pender Islands

Bays and Beaches

 North and South Pender Islands, with some 1,500
permanent residents, encompass a total of 34 square
kilometres. Much of the islands can be toured by car and boat and a
45-kilometre drive around the major roads can be completed in a couple
of hours. But there are so many side roads, isolated coves and beautiful
beaches to explore that even a full weekend is not ample time for a good
look at the Penders.

These islands are joined by a highway bridge which spans a canal
between Bedwell and Browning harbours. Until 1903, when the canal was
excavated, island pioneers were forced to lug their boats laboriously over

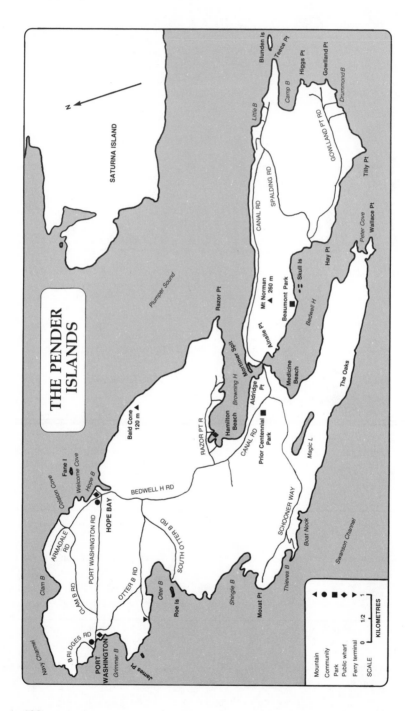

THE PENDER ISLANDS

a wide land neck known as the Indian Portage. There was a great deal of social contact before the turn of the century between islanders at Port Browning and those who lived on the bluffs overlooking Swanson Channel, an area known as The Oaks, which was occasionally used for target practice by British and Italian warships.

Boats, of course, were the major mode of transportation, and as the islands' population grew the residents persuaded the federal government to dredge the ditch between the two islands. Roads were eventually pushed through the wilderness, and in 1955 the provincial government built the bridge, providing both land and ocean travel between the Penders.

These two islands are probably best known for their numerous bays and beaches. Unlike some of the other Gulf Islands served by ferries, most of the tiny coves along the Penders' 61 kilometres of shoreline are accessible by public right of ways. Many of these gravelly beaches are fairly secluded, quiet picnic spots. Canoes and cartoppers can be packed down some public paths and launched from the beaches. A small, easily portaged boat should be a high priority on the Penders for poking around the sheltered nooks and islets.

Many of the places on and around the Penders take their names from early settlers and officers of the Royal Navy. Port Washington on Grimmer Bay, for example, was named after Washington Grimmer, the island's first postmaster. He journeyed regularly by rowboat to Mayne Island to pick up the mail until 1891, when the government wharf was built. Hope Bay is named for Rutherford Hope, a Pender Island farmer who reportedly lived in the first house built on the island, although he was not the first pioneer. Three other familiar Pender island names come from officers of the British naval surveying ship *Plumper*. Pender itself is named for Daniel Pender, who arrived on this coast as second master on the *Plumper*. Bedwell Harbour is named after Edward Parker Bedwell, and Gowlland Point is named in honour of John Thomas Gowlland, both of whom also served as second masters aboard the *Plumper*.

Only about 10 per cent of the Penders' residents live on South Pender, and even with construction of the bridge from North Pender in 1955 there was no great influx of people to South Pender. Many of the Penders' residents live in and around Magic Lake Estates, a subdivision on North Pender's southwest end. This area was originally subdivided by a Vancouver firm in the late 1960s and early '70s.

The creation of Magic Lake Estates triggered a bitter controversy regarding land development on the Penders, which eventually spread to other Gulf Islands. Fears of an unwanted development boom became a concern of all islanders, and the people of the islands demanded some form of control over land and land use. A few years later the Islands Trust, described in Chapter 1, was formed.

North Pender's original settlements — Port Washington, Otter Bay, Hope Bay and Port Browning — have continued to grow, but at a significantly slower pace than Magic Lake. These older communities, with their aging homesteads and cottages, orchards and gardens, are the old side of the Penders, a stark contrast to the contemporary home designs and freshly landscaped lots of the newer developments. Both are interesting to see: they provide some insight into the past and an indication of what the future may hold for the Gulf Islands.

A Route to Follow

A trip around the Penders begins at Otter Bay, as ferries from both sides of Georgia Strait land at this terminal. Follow Otter Bay Road from the terminal to Port Washington, where you can either turn right onto Port Washington Road or continue a few metres to the government wharf on Grimmer Bay.

There is a quaintness to Port Washington similar to that of Vesuvius Bay on Saltspring Island. Old and tidy cottages are clustered around the shores of Grimmer Bay, many with large orchards and neatly trimmed lawns. Boat Islets, in the centre of the bay, can keep a youngster busy most of an afternoon if a boat or raft to get to them is handy.

Port Washington Road leaves the community and heads toward Hope Bay and South Pender. A short distance out of Port Washington there is a turnoff on Clam Bay Road. It is a casual drive through forests of big cedars, firs and maples, particularly colourful in autumn. Toward the end of Clam Bay Road the evergreens give way to deciduous trees as the road meanders past Welcome Cove and Fane Island to Hope Bay, a village about the size of Port Washington.

Just as Port Washington brings memories of Vesuvius, Hope Bay is mildly similar to some parts of Denman Island, an island in Georgia Strait about 130 kilometres northwest of the Gulf Islands. Distinctive wood-sided mansions, the type found in long-established communities, arouse the curiosity of history buffs.

Beyond Hope Bay, Bedwell Harbour Road passes open fields and pastoral sheep farms, spotted with graying, dilapidated barns and outbuildings. You may see as many as a dozen bald eagles in these fields on stormy days when they squat in the open, wings tightly tucked at their sides, facing the wind.

A cemetery, surrounded by Douglas firs, is across Bedwell Harbour Road from one particularly scenic farm, known as Ross-Smith Farm. There is a graveyard on Galiano Island which looks much the same. Both are resting places of Gulf Island pioneers and many of the names on the headstones — Grimmer, Hope, Percival, Hamilton — are known to modern-day islanders as places on Gulf Island maps.

As you come down a steep, winding hill to the Driftwood Centre, the Penders' main shopping complex, you will see signs indicating Browning Harbour Marina. The road to the marina leads to Hamilton Beach, a long and lovely sand and gravel beach with good summer swimming. It is an interesting beach to comb after a winter storm. The beach is named after Alexander Hamilton, a Scottish immigrant who was so enthralled by the scenery of the harbour that he pre-empted a quarter-section of land at the head of the bay in 1885.

Ferry passes Welcome Cove.

The road continues to South Pender, but a short distance before the bridge between the Penders there is a turnoff to Magic Lake Estates. If you take this turn, you will see a sign pointing to a public beach access almost immediately after turning toward Magic lake. This lane is a route to Medicine Beach, a beach at the head of Bedwell Harbour which is much like Hamilton Beach, but not as heavily used.

You can follow Schooner Way to Magic Lake Estates and stop for a dip in the lake. If you continue beyond Magic Lake you will eventually arrive at Thieves Bay, where a public park with picnic tables is located at the edge of a sandy shore. There is a private marina with a breakwater at Thieves Bay. Anglers often find success spincasting off the breakwater.

An extensive network of roads covers this area, but to reach South Pender you must return along Schooner Way toward the bridge. Across the bridge is a sharp left turn down a short, steep hill to Mortimer Spit. The spit forms one side of Shark Cove and is a pretty spot for a swim or to pluck crabs from the sandy bottom. The spit is a narrow arm of grass and sand, a favourite resting spot for cyclists touring the islands.

It is also the site of a bloody murder which ended in death at the gallows for three Cowichan Indians. The year was 1863 and two men sailing the islands stopped for the night on the spit. A party of Indians — three men and two women — arrived and were welcomed by the campers, who offered tea and food. When the men retired after dark the Indians fired guns through the tent, killing one man and wounding the other, who, despite his injuries, managed to scare off the murderers.

He reported the brutal event to authorities in Victoria, who ended their investigation with the arrests of three Indian men and one woman at Chemainus on Vancouver Island. The men were hanged and the woman, reputed to have instigated the slaughter, was sentenced to life in prison.

Cyclists at Mortimer Spit.

Canal Road runs along the north side of South Pender toward Spalding Road. Turn right on Spalding and head toward Bedwell Harbour. You can either drive down to the harbour's edge or turn left on Gowlland Point Road and follow it to a gravel beach lined with driftwood logs. The beach at Gowlland Point is one of the prettiest on South Pender, easily accessible by car or bicycle. The point is a long, grass-covered peninsula jutting into Boundary Pass toward the Canadian-American border. At low tide you can climb into shallow caverns which have been carved by tidal erosion. There are good views of other Gulf Islands and the American San Juan Islands.

There is no circular route which can be taken back to the ferry terminal, and the simplest way to return is by backtracking to North Pender and turning off Bedwell Harbour Road onto Otter Bay Road.

What the Main Route Misses

There are at least five other accessible beaches on the Penders which can be found by following the same route and taking short side trips off the main roads. Many of these beaches are small and used mainly by islanders, but they are public and anyone is welcome to visit them. Pender Island residents have taken the trouble to mark clearly and maintain accesses to their beaches.

Bridges Road

A tiny alcove on the north side of Grimmer Bay can be reached by driving to Port Washington and turning up Bridges Road on the right. The road runs up a hill from the village and follows a ridge above the bay before descending to a short access path to the beach. The cove is a hangout for mink, which can occasionally be spied scampering across the logs. It faces on to Swanson Channel, which is a main route for inter-island and Tsawwassen-Swartz Bay ferries.

Colston Cove

Colston Cove is a rocky shore facing Navy Channel and Mayne Island. There are views of nearby Fane Island and many of the islands between Mayne and Saturna. It is reached by turning left off Clam Bay Road onto Armadale Road and right down a narrow blind road to a stairway which leads to the beach. There are some domestic geese which live in the area and often swim in the bay.

Razor Point

Razor Point Road, off Bedwell Harbour Road across from the Driftwood Centre, runs along the north side of Browning Harbour and leads to a government wharf. A small gravel beach near the wharf is a good picnic and summer swimming spot.

Little Bay

This cove, as the name implies, is a little bay which looks across the open waters of Plumper Sound to bold and barren Brown Ridge on Saturna Island. It can be reached by crossing the bridge to South Pender and following Canal Road to the end. Continue onto Boundary Pass Drive and make a left turn on Conery Crescent. The beach is a few metres along Conery Crescent.

Drummond Bay and Tilly Point

Two roads which run south off Gowlland Point Road lead to worthwhile places to explore. Higgs Road ends at Drummond Bay, where a rock and gravel beach forms a semi-circle around some reefs close to shore. Craddock Drive passes a wide field of broom and provides access to Tilly Point, a well-known scuba-diving area.

Permanently parked at Razor Point.

Transportation

B.C. ferries land on the Penders at Otter Bay. Check telephone directories for airlines and water taxis serving the Penders. Local business operators can provide information about buses, taxis, and car and bicycle rentals.

Emergencies and Information

Dial 911 in an emergency on the Pender Islands. There is a medical clinic and RCMP detachment on North Pender.

Tourist information can be provided by local business and resort operators.

Camping and Accommodation

Prior Centennial Provincial Park is located a short distance from Hamilton Beach, before the turnoff to Magic Lake Estates. It is a 16-hectare campground with 11 sites and a trail to a viewpoint over Browning Harbour. Both Hamilton and Medicine beaches are within walking distance of the park.

Beaumont Provincial Marine Park, on South Pender Island, encompasses much of the shoreline on the north side of Bedwell Harbour. It is accessible by water and can be reached in a rowboat, canoe or kayak from Mortimer Spit, or from the docks at the end of Spalding Road. The park totals 34 wooded hectares and is one of the most popular marine parks in the Gulf Islands. There are 11 campsites and water is available.

The best source for information on private campgrounds, resorts, lodges, or bed-and-breakfasts is Tourism B.C.'s *Accommodations* booklet, described in Chapter 1.

Shopping and Services

The Penders' main shopping area is the Driftwood Centre, a modern complex on Bedwell Harbour Road across from Razor Point Road. There are other commercial outlets on the islands. Pender Islanders are well served with a post office, pubs, liquor outlets, grocery stores, laundromats, service stations, real estate offices, customs facilities, marinas, churches, restaurants and more.

There are service clubs on the islands as well as a variety of studios and galleries which exhibit and sell the works of local artists.

Recreation and Events

Islanders can tell you the whereabouts of tennis courts on the Penders, and there is a golf course on Otter Bay Road. The Pender Island Yacht Club, with headquarters at Thieves Bay, often holds sailing regattas. Check with locals for information on boat, canoe or kayak rentals, bicycle rentals, tours and events.

Pender Islands Hiking — Old Roads and Trails

Some of the hikes on the Penders follow old logging roads to high points on the islands. Many of the roads used for day-to-day travel, such as Razor Point Road, Canal Road, Gowlland Point Road or Clam Bay Road, are pleasant places to walk without venturing too far from civilization.

Mount Norman

The Capital Regional District, which encompasses Greater Victoria and the Gulf Islands, is developing a new 101-hectare park on Mount Norman during the 1990s, with parking facilities and trails to the 260-metre summit. The new park, centred around the Penders' highest point, adjoins Beaumont Provincial Marine Park.

Mount Norman can also be reached from Beaumont Park, up a steep, slippery track through the woods. There are spectacular views of the islands between the Penders and Swartz Bay, the entrance to Bedwell Harbour and the northern San Juan Islands in the United States. Directly below the peak, you can see the Skull Islets and the minuscule shapes of boats moored at Beaumont Park.

Canoeing and Small Boating — Myriad Coves and Islets

Any boater or canoeist travelling aboard a ferry from Tsawwassen or Swartz Bay will immediately feel the urge to take to the sea as the ship approaches Otter Bay, on the west end of North Pender. From Stanley Point on the northwest tip of the island to Mouat Point on the southwest, there are no fewer than 15 coves and half a dozen islets to investigate.

North Pender's Western and Southern Shores

Distance: 16 nautical miles return. *Launching:* Port Washington wharf for canoes or cartoppers.

There are numerous coves and islets between Port Washington and Wallace Point at North Pender's most easterly end, but the waters of Swanson Channel can be dangerous to small craft. The distance from Stanley Point to Wallace Point is 8.5 miles and you could cruise around Wallace Point into Bedwell Harbour. The most fascinating shoreline in this area, however, is between Stanley and Mouat points, a distance of only four miles.

You can hug the shoreline around James Point from Grimmer Gay. As you enter Otter Bay, keep an eye out for ferries and stay out of their way. Beyond the ferry terminal you can slip into Hyashi Cove and continue around the head of the bay, past Roe Islet into Ella Bay. You will pass Irene and Shingle bays on the way to Mouat Point, and if the weather is calm, you can travel down the south side of the island to Thieves Bay and Boat Nook.

The shore rises beyond Boat Nook, peaking to 120 metres at The Oaks, then dropping back to sea level near Smugglers Nook and Peter Cove. Smugglers Nook was once a rendezvous point for rumrunners transporting their wares over the nearby Canadian-American border. Anyone running alongside the edge of The Oaks in a small boat should be wary of weather and marine traffic, remembering there are few places to pull out for about three miles.

River otters, often seen by boaters.

North Pender's Northeast Side

Distance: variable. *Launching:* Hope Bay government wharf or Hamilton Beach.

There is good water for small boats between Hope Bay and Colston Cove but tides, which ebb to the east and flood to the west here, run up to three knots. Flood tides occasionally meet tides flowing north through Plumper Sound, causing rips which may be hazardous to small boats.

Hope Bay is a good launching spot for boaters taking off on camping trips around Plumper Sound. You can travel from Hope Bay across Navy Channel to Mayne Island and along the south side of Mayne toward Saturna. Follow the shorelines between Mayne and Saturna islands, an intriguing area which is described in greater detail in the chapter on Saturna Island. A cruise from Croker Point on Saturna, across Plumper Sound and around the eastern tip of South Pender takes you into Bedwell Harbour. You can then run through the gap between the Penders and up the northeast side of North Pender to Hope Bay.

BROWNING AND BEDWELL HARBOURS

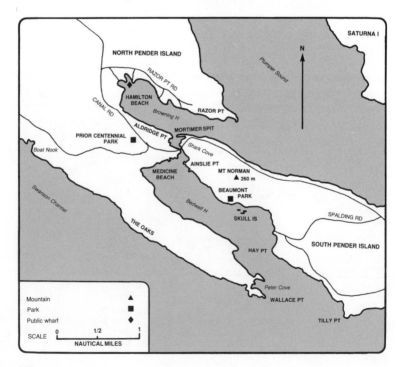

Browning and Bedwell Harbours

Distance: eight nautical miles. *Launching:* Port Browning government wharf or Hamilton Beach.

Hamilton Beach or the government wharf at Port Browning make good starting points for an eight-mile journey through some of the most attractive waters around the Penders. Follow the shoreline along the head of the harbour and down the forested south side toward Aldridge Point and Shark Cove. If the tide is right, you can pass under the bridge into Bedwell Harbour and travel along the head of the bay, past a couple of small coves and around an islet, to Medicine Beach. From the beach it is a 2.5-mile run along the south shore to Peter Cove.

Cross the entrance to Bedwell Harbour to the light at Hay Point and cruise around the point to the docks at the foot of Spalding Road. The run back to Browning Harbour follows the shore of Beaumont Marine Park and continues around Ainslie Point and through the canal.

Browning and Bedwell harbours were once the foraging grounds for an American thief who made annual trips to the Penders to smuggle sheep fleeces. Darkly dressed and under cover of night, he would sneak into the harbours in a rowboat and prowl about the Pender Island storage sheds. He would gather up the fleeces and slip across the border to the San Juan Islands.

American authorities became suspicious when it was reported that a scrubby little rock of an island in the San Juans was Washington State's best wool producer. Fleeces from South Pender were then marked and American officers began night surveillance of their suspect. The South Pender fleeces were eventually found on the San Juan Islands, in the hands of the American smuggler.

When You Arrive by Private Boat

Otter Bay

Otter Bay is not generally used as an anchorage due to wash from the ferries, but Hyashi Cove, on the north side of the bay, offers some protection from ferry wash. There may be moorage and other facilities for boaters at Hyashi Cove.

Bedwell Harbour

Bedwell Harbour is a busy port, with commercial outlets and Beaumont Marine Park attracting boaters from both sides of the border. Peter Cove, at the eastern tip of North Pender, is often used as a temporary anchorage, but most boaters prefer the sheltered waters near the park.

Beaumont Marine Park.

Several mooring buoys are available in the park and the three main beaches are similar to others in the harbour. Eagles, kingfishers, river otters and seals are common sights around Skull Islets, near the eastern end of the park. A trail through the park follows much of the shoreline on the north side of Bedwell Harbour. It's a good place to drop children ashore, with camping gear, so parents can enjoy some peace and privacy aboard their boats.

Browning Harbour and Shark Cove

The clearance under the bridge between the Penders at high water is 8.4 metres (28 feet as shown on the chart) and the width of the canal here is 12 metres. Tides run up to four knots and the canal is best negotiated at slack water. There is good anchorage at Shark Cove, and though southeast winds can blow into Browning Harbour, there are a government wharf and Browning Harbour Marina for moorage. The marina has a full range of facilities for boating families.

Hope Bay

Hope Bay is a tidy little community with a government wharf and a few buildings above the docks. It makes a nice, quiet overnight stop away from the more crowded anchorages at Bedwell and Browning harbours. There's pleasant walking around Hope Bay, and Colston Cove can be reached by foot from the wharf.

Port Washington

There's a government wharf at Port Washington, with a few buildings above. There are several good places to walk around the community, including the Stanley Point-George Hill area where there are nearly six hectares of public land to explore. It can be reached by walking up Bridges Road to Stanley Point Drive.

Pender Islands Fishing — Salmon, Cod and Trout

The Penders are not known for fantastic fishing, but there are a few spots which generally produce better than others. Many Pender Islanders prefer to run to the fishier waters at East Point and Active Pass.

Wallace Point

Launching: Bedwell Harbour or Otter Bay.

Wallace Point, at the eastern end of North Pender, often yields spring salmon in the five- to ten-pound range. It is generally deep-water fishing and the most successful fishermen are those who troll off the end of the point or along the edge of The Oaks on the south side of the island. Boaters staying overnight in Bedwell Harbour often congregate off Wallace Point to drift fish on summer evenings.

Tilly and Gowlland Points

Launching: Bedwell Harbour.

The stretch of water between these two points, off the southeast end of South Pender, offers catches similar to those taken off Wallace Point. The underwater ledges shown on hydrographic charts guide fishermen to the appropriate depths for salmon and ling cod. Tidal flows off Gowlland Point are often swift, and spincasting off the tip of the point catches the odd cod or salmon for anglers willing to risk getting snagged on the rocks.

Magic Lake

Rumour has it that lunker trout lurk in the depths of Magic Lake and they rise to a fly in early morning and late evening.

Pender Islands Scuba Diving

Tilly Point

Shore dive — off rocks at end of Craddock Drive.

The most popular scuba-diving waters of the Penders are at Tilly Point on the southeast end of South Pender. The point can be reached by driving east on Gowlland Point Road and turning left onto Craddock Drive. Tilly Point is known among divers for its eerie underwater caverns which extend three to five metres into the rocky shoreline at a depth of eight or nine metres.

Seaside life on the Penders.

After the Penders, What Next?

The Penders are the most populated of the outer islands and because they are reasonably close to Vancouver Island, a small number of the residents are able to commute daily to Victoria. Galiano, Mayne and Saturna, however, are not within commuting distance, and if you travel on to these outer islands, you will find fewer people, fewer facilities, and an even greater sense of isolation.

<u>Galiano</u>

An Island That
Leaves an Indelible Impression

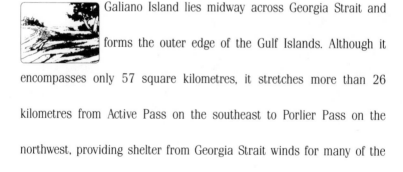Galiano Island lies midway across Georgia Strait and forms the outer edge of the Gulf Islands. Although it encompasses only 57 square kilometres, it stretches more than 26 kilometres from Active Pass on the southeast to Porlier Pass on the northwest, providing shelter from Georgia Strait winds for many of the other islands.

Galiano, the driest of all the Gulf Islands, receives less than 60 centimetres of rainfall a year. About half of the land is owned by MacMillan Bloedel, British Columbia's forestry giant. Most of Galiano's 800-odd permanent residents are concentrated on the south end, between Sturdies

119

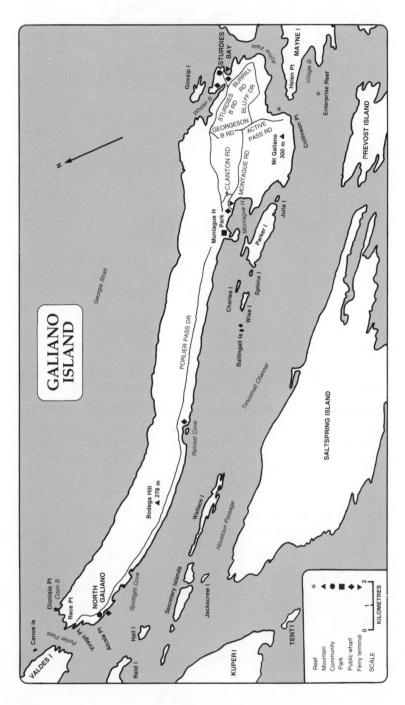

GALIANO ISLAND

Bay and Montague Harbour, and a few tiny residential communities are scattered along the southern side of the island as far as Porlier Pass. Many of these residents are retired, some work in tourism and service industries, and a few are writers and artists.

Many people who make a habit of touring the Gulf Islands consider Galiano the most scenic of the entire group. From the bluffs at the southeastern end to the low-lying points jutting into Porlier Pass, there is an idyllic charm to Galiano that sets it apart from other pretty places along the B.C. coast. A weekend or a day-trip to the island is a pleasant journey, regardless of season, and most highlights can be seen by driving or cycling a total of about 65 kilometres from the ferry terminal at Sturdies Bay.

A Route to Follow

After disembarking from the ferry at Sturdies Bay, drive up from the terminal and turn left on Burrill Road. Follow Burrill to a point where it takes a sharp bend up Bluff Drive, a good stop for views of ferries in Active Pass. Bluff Drive is a good gravel road which climbs above the edge of Georgeson Bay toward Galiano Bluffs. The three-kilometre journey along Bluff Drive from Burrill Road meanders through old, dark forests of fir and cedar to Georgeson Bay Road.

Turn right onto Georgeson Bay Road, then left on Montague Harbour Road. Turn right onto Clanton Road and left on Porlier Pass Drive, the only route to the northwest end of Galiano Island. Porlier Pass Drive runs about

Lighthouse Bay on Porlier Pass.

23 kilometres beside Trincomali Channel to Lighthouse Bay. There are viewpoints overlooking the waterways and islands between Galiano and Vancouver Island.

Though the route to the northwest tip of Galiano is long and straight, it is by no means tedious. Shortly after turning onto Porlier Pass Drive, you will climb a point high above Montague Harbour where some power lines cross the road. You can walk under the power lines and stand at the edge of a sheer bluff which drops more than 100 metres to Montague Harbour. From the point you can watch boats steaming in and out of the bay below while eagles drift on the wind at eye level.

The ridges along the right side of the road as you travel toward Porlier Pass maintain a constant height of 180 metres between the viewpoint above Montague Harbour and a turnoff to Retreat Cove. The ridges are sheer and so close to the road that they block out the early morning sun. Beyond the turnoff to Retreat Cove the road gradually drops to a level of about 35 metres and continues toward the northwest, with Trincomali Channel on the left and the 240-metre peak of Bodega Hill looming on the right. It finally descends to sea level a short distance before Spotlight Cove and hugs the shore all the way to Porlier Pass.

As Porlier Pass Drive is the only route to the northwest end, you must follow it all the way back to the intersection at Georgeson Bay Road and turn onto Sturdies Bay Road to reach the ferry terminal.

What the Main Route Misses

By following the same route around Galiano and taking short jaunts off the main roads you will find a number of bays and beaches, sights and viewpoints.

Bellhouse Park

On the south side of Sturdies Bay is Burrill Point, reached by turning left on Burrill road and left again on Jack Road. The point is the site of Bellhouse Park, a rocky, moss-covered peninsula which slopes gently to the sea at the northeast entrance to Active Pass. A few picnic tables are the only park facilities. Tides run up to five knots off the park and the shoreline drops sharply into deep water, making it an excellent spincasting point for cod and salmon. Directly across the channel is Active Pass Light Station on Mayne Island, with the snowy peak of Mount Baker, in the state of Washington, in the background.

Galiano Bluffs Park

Galiano Bluffs, which rise 120 metres above Active Pass, are an excellent vantage point for views over the southwest end of the pass and down Swanson Channel toward the Penders, Prevost and Saltspring islands, and Swartz Bay on Vancouver Island. As Active Pass is the busiest waterway in the Gulf Islands, it is virtually impossible to watch the waters from Galiano Bluffs Park, a local park, without seeing vessels either approaching or leaving the pass.

The route to the bluffs is a short lane to the left as you head along Bluff Drive toward Georgeson Bay Road. The road is skirted by huge western red cedars, giving way to Douglas firs near the summit where some of the oldest trees in the Gulf Islands have been mercifully spared from the woodsman's axe.

Active Pass Road

For a sea-level look at ships running down Active Pass toward Vancouver Island, Active Pass Road, a short jaunt to the left at the end of Bluff Drive, ends at a small cemetery on the shore of Georgeson Bay. The marker on Collinson Reef, where the ferry *Queen of Alberni* ran aground in the summer of 1979, stands a few metres from the beach. Seals and seabirds often feed in kelp beds around the reef. Ships run directly at the

View from Bellhouse Park.

reef before making a sharp turn to the end of Active Pass between Collinson and Helen points.

The graveyard, with meticulously clipped lawns and fresh flowers, is the burial place of several early Galiano settlers. Many of the names found on nautical charts and topographic maps of the Gulf Islands are carved

Montague Harbour Park.

on weatherbeaten tombstones — Georgeson, Burrill, Scoones, Drummond and others.

Montague Harbour Park

Montague Harbour Provincial Park, totalling 87 hectares, is the most popular marine park in the Gulf Islands. It has two campgrounds, one for boaters and bicyclists, another for motorists. Its shell and gravel beaches are safe swimming spots for kids and the sheltered harbour is ideal for young rowers. Gray Peninsula, inhabited by Indians for about 3,000 years before the arrival, in 1792, of the Spanish Explorer Dionisio Alcala Galiano, is part of the park. Shell beaches on either side of an isthmus joining the peninsula to the campground are good spots for picnics and general loafing. A wharf divides the beach in half and a lagoon on the isthmus separates the two main beaches in the park. A launching ramp is located in the park and there are two caves along the southern shore of Galiano on the western side of the park. They can be reached by foot at low tide, or by boat.

Retreat Cove

About 12 kilometres along Porlier Pass Drive there is a turnoff to Retreat Cove, a tiny bay with a government wharf and an island just off the shore. Otters play around the wharf and eagles roost in the trees on the island. A grass-covered, rocky point above the wharf faces the island and offers good views, across Trincomali Channel, of Wallace and Saltspring islands. The cove is used occasionally by paddlers as a departure point for expeditions around the Secretary Island group, which is described in the chapter on Saltspring Island.

Whaler Bay and Cain Peninsula

Whaler Bay, once used as an anchorage for small whaling boats, is a sheltered enclave protected from Georgia Strait seas by Gossip Island and Cain Peninsula. A government wharf is located at the end of a road off Cain Road.

Cain Peninsula is one of the south-end population centres and has a number of large, old waterfront homes and modern seaside cottages. Cain Road ends abruptly at a dead end, where a path leads to a rock and gravel beach with long sandstone fingers reaching into Georgia Strait. The beach is piled high with driftwood logs, a good place to sit and watch traffic entering Active Pass from Georgia Strait.

Transportation

Sturdies Bay is the is the Galiano terminus for all B.C. ferries. Check tourist centres or telephone directories for information on air services, water taxis, buses, taxis, and car and bicycle rentals.

Emergencies and Information

In an emergency on Galiano get to a phone and dial 911. The Saltspring Island RCMP detachment is responsible for policing Galiano.

A Travel Infocentre may operate at Sturdies Bay. Check telephone directories for a phone number. Local businesses and resorts can answer questions from tourists.

Camping and Accommodation

The only provincial campsites are at Montague Harbour Park. Located at the end of Montague Harbour Road, the park is used by boaters, backpackers and bicyclists from Vancouver Island and the mainland. There are two campgrounds — one for boaters and bicyclists, another for vehicles — with a total of 40 campsites.

There are lodges, resorts, inns, and bed-and-breakfast establishments on Galiano. For up-to-date listings, check the local chamber of commerce or Tourism B.C.'s annual *Accommodations* booklet, described in Chapter 1.

Shopping and Services

Sturdies Bay is the main business centre, with real estate offices, a liquor outlet, stores, restaurants, service stations, post office and other amenities. Locals can provide information on pubs, churches, eateries, service clubs, marinas, and other attractions on the island. Like other Gulf Islands, Galiano is inhabited by several talented artists whose work can be viewed and purchased at various outlets.

Recreation and Events

Galiano has a golf course and tennis courts. Check the Travel Infocentre or local businesses for details on rentals of bicycles, boats, canoes or kayaks, fishing and cruising charters, guided nature tours, diving adventures and other Galiano activities. There are a number of annual sales, art exhibitions, festivals and celebrations.

Galiano Island Hiking — Beaches and Coves

Dionisio Point and Coon Bay

A trail along the shore of Porlier Pass leads to Race Point Lighthouse and a series of coves on the northwest end of Galiano to Dionisio Point and Coon Bay. To get to Lighthouse Bay, go to the Indian reserve at the end of Porlier Pass Drive. The trail begins past a house at the end of the road and permission is required to cross in front of the house. Take the trail to a clearing where a sign points down a dirt road to Coon Bay; ignore the road and take the trail, marked by a sign pointing out the route to Race Point Lighthouse.

It is about a 45-minute walk along an intricate shoreline, with several sunny beaches facing Porlier Pass, to Coon Bay, possibly the most beautiful corner of Galiano Island. At Coon Bay a narrow isthmus with sandy beaches

DIONISIO POINT AND COON BAY

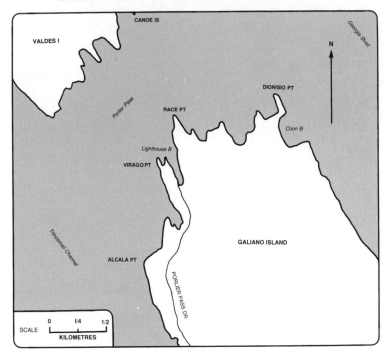

Spincasting at Dionisio Point.

on either side connects a tree-covered islet at low tide. Flat sandstone ledges, similar to some on the West Coast Trail of Pacific Rim National Park, can be hiked around the islet.

Coon Bay is an extraordinarily scenic seascape, with sandy beaches on both sides of the isthmus and unimpaired views of Porlier Pass and Valdes Island. There are two other good beaches along the seaside trail from Lighthouse Bay. The hike to Coon Bay is the only excuse necessary for a trip to Galiano Island.

Canoeing and Small Boating — Offshore Islets and Islands

Montague Harbour

Distance: nine nautical miles. *Launching:* Montague Harbour Park.

Montague Harbour Park is a favourite home base for paddlers and small boaters navigating the surrounding channels and shorelines. Montague Harbour itself makes an interesting one-hour row or paddle and the islands and islets outside the harbour are sheltered enough for small boats.

Parker Island lies at the gateway to the harbour, protecting both Montague Harbour and a narrow channel which leads into the harbour. A circumnavigation of a group of privately owned islands, including Parker, Julia, Sphinx, Charles and Wise islands, takes two or three hours from Montague Harbour Park.

Ballingall Islets, at the northwestern end of the chain, are an intriguing destination. The islets are among a few Gulf Island landmarks where cormorants nest in trees. More than 30 double-crested cormorants have built stick nests in the tops of short, Rocky Mountain juniper trees, a rather surprising but humorous sight for unsuspecting yachtsmen.

Retreat Cove and Island

Distance: one nautical mile. *Launching:* government wharf.

Retreat Cove is a nice setting for a leisurely row on a sunny afternoon, when you feel like being away from the people at Montague Harbour or the more populated lower end of Galiano. Chances of seeing eagles, otters, sea lions or harbour seals are good, and there are a few places where you might want to offer a hook and mussel to a rock cod or perch.

Gossip Island

Distance: 1.5 nautical miles. *Launching:* Cain Peninsula.

Gossip Island, another sheltered paddling area, lies off Cain Peninsula, protecting Whaler Bay from Georgia Strait winds. Canoes or cartoppers can be launched in a bay at the end of Cain Road, or from the government wharf at Whaler Bay, for a trip around Gossip Island and nearby coves, a lazy way to fill the hours while waiting for a ferry at Sturdies Bay.

When You Arrive by Private Boat

Sturdies Bay

There is a small government wharf at Sturdies Bay near the ferry terminal. All of the facilities in the village of Sturdies Bay are within walking distance. Bellhouse Park, a great spot for a picnic or walk, and Cain Peninsula are short strolls from the wharf.

Whaler Bay

Whaler Bay, with a government wharf on the western side, is sheltered from all but northerly winds. A number of coves around the shores of the

Nesting cormorants.

bay are good anchorages but the entrance to the bay is reef-strewn, so be careful when approaching it.

The bay is often used by boaters waiting for tide in Active Pass and there are several places — Cain Peninsula, Sturdies Bay, Bellhouse Park — to explore while you are there. The golf course is less than three kilometres from the east side of the bay.

Porlier Pass

Currents flood up to nine knots and ebb up to eight knots to Porlier Pass, and high seas can build when flood tides meet oncoming northerly winds. This pass should be entered as close as possible to slack water and special attention should be given to the rocks and reefs shown on the charts.

Coon Bay dries at low tide, but there is protection from southeasterlies in the bay to the west of Dionisio Point. Lighthouse Bay offers similar shelter. This area is probably the most scenic part of Galiano Island and is described in the hiking section of this chapter.

North Galiano

A government wharf is located at North Galiano but is open to most winds. It is not an especially good overnight stop but is a pretty place for a walk along the edge of Trincomali Channel.

Whaler Bay.

Retreat Cove

There is a government wharf at Retreat Cove but the bay is exposed to westerly winds. You can drop anchor on the east and west sides of Retreat Island but the water behind it is dangerously shallow. A walk up Retreat Cove is a relaxing way to wait out a storm, and the point overlooking the bay is a pleasant place to perch and catch a few sunrays.

Montague Harbour

Montague Harbour is one of the prettiest, and therefore one of the busiest, ports in the southern Gulf Islands. Montague Harbour Park, on the western side of the bay, has a wharf and several mooring buoys, and there is plenty of room to drop the hook within dinghy distance of the beach.

Some moorage is available at a government wharf and the harbour is fairly protected from all sides: you can anchor in virtually any part of the bay. The eastern end is usually less crowded than the park, and there are several interesting old cottages overlooking the beaches, a nice place to row in the evenings.

There are bays on the east and west sides of Parker Island, which forms the southern side of the harbour, that can be used for overnight moorage away from the crowds. Prevost Island, a popular meeting place for Gulf Island boaters, has numerous protected anchorages and is a three-mile cruise across Trincomali Channel from the entrance to Montague Harbour.

Galiano Island Fishing — Two Productive Passes

Galiano Island lies between Porlier Pass and Active Pass, two of the hottest salmon-fishing spots in the Gulf Islands. Both places are well known to anglers from Vancouver Island, and fishermen from the mainland think nothing of running across Georgia Strait in small boats to get a piece of the action around Galiano Island. A detailed look at Active Pass is provided in Chapter 1.

Helen Point

Launching: Montague Harbour Park.

Fisheries officers who patrol Active Pass say there is no question that Active Pass provides the best summer fishing in the Gulf Islands. However, keep well out of the way of the ferries. Spring and coho salmon migrating to spawning grounds in the Fraser and other mainland and Vancouver Island rivers swim through Active Pass and feed on resident herring.

Most of the fishing at the southwest entrance is concentrated around Helen Point, on Mayne Island, where back eddies form around the point on the ebb tide. Mooching with live herring or cut plugs is the technique used by most fishermen here, but many use drift-fishing lures such as stingsildas or pirkens. Trolling the shorelines between Helen Point and Village Bay on Mayne, or near Collinson Point on Galiano, is usually productive and often done by fishermen with sailboats, without enough power and manoeuvrability to handle the swift currents inside the pass.

Miners Bay

Launching: Montague Harbour Park.

Miners Bay, midway through the pass, has a circular tidal flow and fishermen troll in circles around the bay. It is a good spot to fish deep for winter springs. Sizeable salmon are also taken off the government wharf here by spincasters.

Georgina Point

Launching: Montague Harbour Park.

The methods used off Georgina Point are similar to those used at the opposite end of the pass, but this area is fished on the flood tide. There is more area to fish here, as the channel is wider than at the other end, and there is good fishing along the shorelines of both Mayne and Galiano islands. Many anglers troll and drift fish around Georgina Shoals and at Gossip Island on the other side of Active Pass. This area is not as restricted as the southwest entrance and there is less chance of getting mowed down by a ferry.

Porlier Pass

Launching: ramp at North Galiano.

Tides run up to nine knots at Porlier Pass and, like Active Pass, are dangerous to underpowered boats. There is excellent mooching and drift fishing at either end of the pass and trollers work the waters off Alcala and Dionisio points. Porlier Pass Marina caters to fishermen, and many anglers set up a base near Coon Bay and stay for a couple of weeks during the peak salmon runs.

Bellhouse Park

Tidal currents off the rocks at Bellhouse Park, on Burrill Point, are swift and make this area a pretty good bet for salmon and cod. Spincasters with fairly heavy lures cast from the rocks and pick up good-sized salmon and lings.

Galiano Island Scuba Diving

The scuba diving on Galiano is the best available on the outer Gulf Islands and many of the good diving spots are near the good fishing areas. There have been air stations on the island in the past, but the availability of air is something which should be checked when making arrangements to visit Galiano.

Alcala Point

Shore dive.

Alcala Point is an underwater photographer's dream. Almost immediately after stepping off the shore you are in a large bed of bull kelp with dozens of big fish swimming among the long, brown streamers and stems. There are lots of anemones of varying colours, rock and swimming scallops, urchins, octopi, huge barnacles and a large assortment of sea stars.

Some divers descend to more than 30 metres here, but there is a great deal to see within the top 12 metres. Tidal currents off Alcala Point reach seven knots and it must be explored at slack water. A knife should be carried in case you run into problems with the kelp.

Virago Point

Shore dive.

The waters of Virago Point, at Porlier Pass near Alcala Point, are good for snorkellers, as much of the marine life is at shallow depths where a rocky bottom gradually descends to a sandy sea floor at about 10 or 12 metres. There is a variety of crabs and anemones, as well as an abundance of rock fish and perch and the odd octopus.

Like Alcala Point, this area should be dived at slack water and a knife should be carried.

Canoe Islet

Boat dive — launching at North Galiano.

In 1868 Canoe Islet, off the southeast end of Valdes Island, became the permanent resting place of the *Del Norte*, a 57-metre passenger steamer which went down in 1868. The rusting hulk was not discovered until 1972, and no recreational divers bothered about it until 1975. There are still dozens of artifacts scattered around the surrounding sea bottom, as well as numerous marine plants and animals. The remains of the *Del Norte* are now protected under the Heritage Conservation Act of B.C.

Currents here are strong.

Active Pass

Boat or shore dive — launching at Montague Harbour Park.

Active Pass is a deep and dangerous dive, to be tackled only by highly experienced divers. Currents are strong and there is a great deal of marine traffic, including fishermen with hazardous lines and hooks. Someone should always remain on the surface when diving Active Pass, and proper diver identification should be clearly visible to other boaters.

The rewards of diving Active Pass, however, are comparable to the dangers. There are thousands of fish anywhere in the pass, beautiful flowering beds of multi-coloured anemones and dozens of kelp beds. Much of the scenery is at more than 30 metres, where giant ling cod and bottomfish linger.

After Galiano, What Next?

Galiano Island shares many of the natural characteristics of other Gulf Islands: sandstone and gravel beaches; forests of Douglas fir, cedar, arbutus and Garry oak; and a certain degree of isolation — not enough for a dedicated hermit, but satisfying to a weekend recluse. And like other Gulf Islands, Galiano possesses an inexplicable distinction, a uniqueness which separates it from the other islands in spite of its similarities. It is an island that entices explorers to visit other islands in the hopes of finding something similar, or possibly discovering something quite different.

<u>Mayne</u>

Something Old, Something New

 Mayne Island is an interesting combination of old and new. From contemporary homes in modern subdivisions of Village Bay to gracious old mansions on the shores of Miners Bay, Mayne is a hundred years of Gulf Island history neatly packaged on one island.

Visitors expecting to find clusters of cozy cottages, smoke spiralling from their chimneys, might be somewhat taken aback upon arrival at the Village Bay ferry terminal, for the streets in the valley at the head of the bay, and on the points above, are newly paved and lined with city-type homes. Yet only two kilometres from Village Bay, some of the first homes built in the Gulf Islands are still standing at Miners Bay.

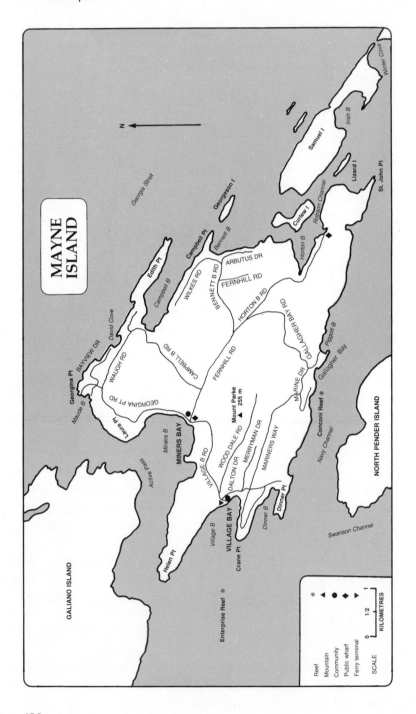

MAYNE ISLAND

There are many places on Mayne Island where turn-of-the-century buildings stand side-by-side with modern-day homes, and most of these areas can be seen on a 30-kilometre tour of the island's main roads. Mayne Island encompasses a total of 21 square kilometres and has a population of about 700. Many live in small centres separated by big, beautiful farms and uninhabited woodlands. It is a cyclist's paradise with long, leisurely country roads, most of them paved, but like other Gulf Islands, Mayne has its fair allotment of hills.

Mayne Island is known for its King apples and is said to have been the first place in British Columbia to grow apples. The story is that an English sea captain bound for the west coast of North America was attending a formal affair before his departure. A lady slipped some apple seeds in his waistcoat pocket, with a suggestion that the captain plant them at his destination. He forgot about the seeds until he was attending another such event on Mayne Island, clad in the same waistcoat. When he reached into his pocket, he discovered the seeds and, remembering the lady's suggestion, planted them on Mayne.

There are numerous orchards on Mayne Island, and though apples were never a major crop, they were one of several grown by pioneer farmers. Many of Mayne's early farmers raised sheep and some later turned to greenhouses. Japanese people became a prominent part of the island's citizenry, and their greenhouse produce and poultry were an integral part of Mayne Island's economy. It was a great loss to all Gulf Islanders when

Fine old home near Campbell Bay.

the Japanese were moved away from the coast to other parts of Canada at the outbreak of World War II.

Tourism was also a factor in the economic well-being of Mayne Island, and the island's nickname, "Little Hell," arises from the number of pubs it had in its formative years. Before the turn of the century, two hotels — Springwater Lodge and the Mayne Island Inn — were in operation at Miners Bay. Another inn, named the Point Comfort Hotel, was built near Georgina Point in the early 1890s by Warburton Pike, a well-known Gulf Island pioneer who also provided the site for St. Mary Magdalene Church at Miners Bay. The Point Comfort Hotel, which later operated under the name Cherry Tree Inn, was demolished in 1958. The Mayne Island Inn was destroyed by fire in 1921.

Many of the island's original farms are operating today, and you will discover large, open fields with sheep or cows lazily grazing around old, tumbledown barns as you travel around. The advent of B.C. ferries and arrival of new inhabitants brought a limited amount of commerce, and quite a few Mayne Islanders are employed today in service industries and businesses which provide for the needs of local people. As on the other Gulf Islands, a large percentage of Mayne Islanders are retired.

Although populations have grown, the primary population centres have not moved. Miners Bay is still the bustling community it was when people gathered at "the Pass" in the late 1800s and early 1900s to wait for the arrival of the mail and supply ships. Village Bay, an Indian village before the coming of white settlers, and Bennett Bay, on the opposite end of the island, are rapidly taking on the aura of suburbia, but some of the original Mayne Island homes remain in these areas today.

Ferry passes Miners Bay.

A Route to Follow

Village Bay is the location of the only ferry terminal on Mayne Island and a good starting point for a tour of the island. Village Bay Road, originally an ox trail, is a narrow, winding highway from the ferry terminal, through forests of cedar and fir, to Miners Bay, a community which derives its name from the Fraser River gold rush of 1858.

When gold was discovered on the Fraser, Miners Bay was inundated with fortune seekers travelling between Vancouver Island and the mainland. The bay is precisely halfway between Vancouver Island and the mouth of the Fraser and was a convenient overnight stop for miners planning to row across Georgia Strait. Literally thousands of treasure hunters passed through Active Pass en route to the gold.

On March 23, 1858, a team of gold miners sifting the gravel at Hill's Bar, 16 kilometres upstream from Hope, hit the first big strike. Within weeks, Fraser River gold fever had become an epidemic, and by autumn 33,000 Americans had reached the Fraser River, many via Miners Bay.

Miners Bay has remained Mayne Island's centre of activity, and although the British Columbia Ferry Corporation built a terminal at Village Bay in the early 1960s, a government wharf at Miners Bay is still a busy stop for various vessels. The "Coronation Tree and Seat" at the head of the wharf was placed there to commemorate the coronation of King George VI of England, on May 12, 1937. It is a pleasant resting spot to spend an hour or two watching ships and ferries steam in and out of Active Pass.

Examples of Mayne Island's 19th-century architecture are found throughout the Miners Bay area. On the main street are the Agricultural Hall, the Island Gaol which now is a museum, and Springwater Lodge, all built at the turn of the century. If you follow Georgina Point Road from the government wharf along the Miners Bay shoreline, you will see a number of elegant old mansions overlooking the bay. St. Mary Magdalene Church, built in 1898, stands in a beautiful setting of arbutus and fir trees above the bay, with a seaside cemetery adjoining the church grounds. Just beyond the church, on the waterfront side of the road, there is a large private home known as The Anchorage which operated as a guest house before World War II.

Follow Georgina Point Road about three kilometres to Waugh Road. Take Waugh about two kilometres to a sharp bend and a short, steep hill at the head of Campbell Bay. From here take Campbell Bay Road.

At the junction of Campbell Bay and Fernhill roads, turn left onto Fernhill toward Bennett Bay. As the road passes Old Fernhill Road, one of Mayne's oldest farms — Hardscrabble Farm — is located on the left; the blue roof of the original farmhouse is visible from the road. Beyond

Hardscrabble Farm, Fernhill Road goes to the right into an area of new homes. Bennett Bay Road begins here, veering to the left. Near Bennett Bay you can turn left onto Wilkes Road; a short distance down Wilkes is a public access to the beautiful sandy shores of the bay. You can also turn right and drive along Arbutus, through an area of new homes, and loop back onto Fernhill Road.

To reach Horton Bay from Bennett Bay, backtrack along Bennett Bay and Fernhill roads then turn left onto Horton Bay Road. Keep to the left at the junction of Horton Bay and Gallagher Bay roads and pass a long driveway, lined with maple trees, which leads to a farmhouse. This farm, established in 1871, is the oldest on Mayne Island. There are a number of rustic cabins and farms, many with orchards, on the road to Horton Bay.

Horton Bay is an extremely protected anchorage and the site of a tiny community of nomadic houseboaters who tow their homes from cove to cove around the Gulf Islands. One or two of these unique floating abodes can usually be seen anchored in the bay or tied to the government wharf. The wharf is a good spot for youngsters to poke around under pilings and a launching spot for canoes and small boats. If you listen carefully you may hear the high-pitched wails of peacocks, which belong to the owners of nearby Curlew Island.

Gallagher Bay is reached by retracing the route from Horton Bay to the junction at Gallagher Bay Road and turning left. Slightly more than two kilometres from the junction, Gallagher Bay Road runs into Piggott Road which spans a headland and joins two bays. Gallagher Bay, on the right, is a small cove on Navy Channel. At the other end of Piggott Road is Piggott Bay, a much larger cove with a beautiful sandy beach facing Plumper Sound and Saturna Island. The beach, lined with driftwood, is shallow and fairly warm for swimming during summer and is a good vantage point for watching eagles and winter storms. Boats can be launched from these beaches, but the ground may be soft and you might have to clear some logs.

As you head out of the Gallagher-Piggott Bay area, turn left off Gallagher Bay Road and keep left onto Marine Drive. At the intersection of Marine Drive and Mariners Way, take Mariners Way toward Village Bay.

There are nice views over the valley at the head of Village Bay as Mariners Way approaches the new developments at Mayne Island's western end. The valley is dominated by Mount Parke, the highest peak on the island. A big white building at the centre of the valley is the original barn of a farm which was built here after the land was pre-empted in 1873. A right turn on Dalton Drive takes you to the ferry terminal.

What the Main Route Misses

There is a variety of sights to be seen on short jaunts off the main route around Mayne Island, including a lighthouse, views over Georgia Strait and beaches.

Georgina Point

Georgina Point is slightly more than three kilometres north of Miners Bay. Follow Georgina Point Road to the intersection at Waugh Road and turn left. The road ends at Active Pass Light Station, the lighthouse seen by passengers aboard ferries as they enter Active Pass from Georgia Strait. The lighthouse, built in 1885, is an interesting stop and is open to visitors between one and three p.m.

Mayne Island is believed to be the only Gulf Island on which Captain George Vancouver landed during a voyage in 1792. Some evidence of early exploration was found at Georgina Point in 1881, when an island pioneer unearthed part of a seaman's knife and an English penny dated 1794.

Cherry Tree Bay

Cherry Tree Bay, officially named Maude Bay, is a small cove with a beach and good summer swimming near the lighthouse. It is located at the end of Cherry Tree Bay Road, a left turn only a few metres before the lighthouse.

Bayview Drive

Bayview Drive is off Bay Road, which is across the road to Georgina Point from Cherry Tree Bay Road. Bay Road ends at a tiny, rock-strewn cove and Bayview continues to the right along the northern side of Mayne Island. There are nice views of Georgia Strait, and Reef Bay Road, a short track off Bayview, leads to a beach facing onto the strait. Bayview ends at the top of a ledge overlooking David Cove, a nice view of the cove but not a good access to the water.

Bennett Bay Beach

The long rock and sand beach at Bennett Bay is the finest on the island and a great spot to laze away a summer afternoon. It is reached by turning left on Wilkes Road as you enter the Bennett Bay area.

There are lots of logs and driftwood for raft building. The water at Bennett Bay is shallow near the shore and good for swimming. There are good views of Georgia Strait, the north end of Curlew Island, and Georgeson Island, a frequent roost for bald eagles.

Dinner Bay Park

When heading toward Village Bay on Mariners Way, continue a short distance past Dalton Road and turn left onto Dinner Bay Road, then right on Williams Place. This is a community park with open grass areas,

Bennett Bay.

washrooms, a barbecue shelter, and stairs to a lovely sand and gravel beach with tide pools at low tides.

Transportation

All B.C. ferries to Mayne Island land at Village Bay. Check telephone directories for air service and water taxis. Local businesses usually know if buses, taxis, car or bicycle rentals are available.

Emergencies and Information

In an emergency on Mayne Island call 911. The island has a medical clinic and laws are enforced by RCMP from the Pender Islands.

There may be a Travel Infocentre at Miners Bay or you can inquire about island facilities and events at the museum or from local businesses. There are bulletin boards at Miners Bay and other commercial areas.

Camping and Accommodation

There are no provincial campgrounds on Mayne. For current information on resorts, lodges, and bed-and-breakfast outlets, check local businesses or Tourism B.C.'s *Accommodations* booklet, described in Chapter 1.

Shopping and Services

Miners Bay is the "downtown" of Mayne Island, with a pub and liquor outlet, post office, real estate offices, restaurants, service station and other necessities of island life. Other commercial outlets are found elsewhere on the island. The artwork of many talented Mayne Islanders is available from stores, studios and galleries throughout the island.

Recreation and Events

There are tennis courts on Mayne, and locals can offer information on sailing, cruising and fishing charters, service clubs and annual events including community fairs, craft sales, salmon barbecues and theatre presentations.

Mayne Island Hiking — Quiet Country Roads

There is no abundance of public hiking trails on Mayne Island, but many of the island's roads are good places to walk. The pace on Mayne Island is slow, and you could spend a long time enjoying the easy, country atmosphere found throughout most of the island.

Crane Point

Mariners Way winds around the end of Crane Point, which forms the south side of Village Bay, and runs into Spinnaker Drive. Spinnaker intersects Dinner Bay Road to form a loop around Crane Point. A stroll around these roads takes about an hour.

Navy Channel Road

At the intersection of Mariners Way and Marine Drive, Marine Drive descends to the left, if you are heading toward Village Bay, and intersects with Navy Channel Road. You can leave a vehicle at the intersection and take a 15-minute walk down the road and along the shores of Navy Channel. From the road there are nice views of North Pender Island, on the opposite side of the channel, and down the side of North Pender toward Plumper Sound.

Edith Point

Slightly more than a kilometre from the beginning of Waugh Road as you head toward Campbell Bay, there is a turnoff to the left on Porter Road. There is access to David Cove here and good walking along Edith Point Road.

Mount Parke

A 31-hectare park, to be developed on Mount Parke, Mayne Island's most prominent landmark, during the 1990s, will include a parking area, access and trails to the mountain.

Satellite radar equipment near Mount Parke's 255-metre peak helps track ship movements on the lower B.C. coast. It is one of several satellite stations which form a vessel traffic management system, with headquarters in West Vancouver. The Mayne station, which is unmanned, records ship movements in the waters between Active Pass and the entrance to Juan de Fuca Strait.

There are exceptional views of Active Pass from the top of the mountain.

Paddling and Small Boating — Open Waters

Village Bay to Dinner Point

Distance: 3.5 nautical miles return. *Launching:* at end of Callaghan Crescent off Mariners Way.

The trip along the shoreline between Village Bay and Dinner Point takes in some scenic, low-lying bluffs and beaches, but it is exposed to wash from ferries travelling in Trincomali and Swanson channels. If the weather is calm you could continue down Navy Channel toward Conconi Reef and Gallagher and Piggott bays.

Horton Bay

Distance: two nautical miles. *Launching:* government wharf.

The waters of Horton Bay are sheltered by Curlew Island and are safe for youngsters who want to poke around in a canoe or rowboat. There are some tidal currents in Robson Channel, but they are stronger on the outside edge of Curlew Island.

Horton Bay.

Bennett Bay

Distance: variable. *Launching:* at end of public access lane off Wilkes road.

Much small-boating water is accessible from Bennett Bay and this beach can be used as the start of a journey between Saturna and Mayne islands, which is described in the chapter on Saturna.

If you launch off the beach, you can travel southeast toward Horton Bay or run northwest around Campbell Point into Campbell Bay. Georgeson Island, off the point, is frequented by eagles and easy to circumnavigate in calm weather. After exploring Campbell Bay, you could continue around Edith Point and along the north side of Mayne as far as David Cove. These waters, however, are exposed and small boaters should keep a watchful eye on weather and sea conditions.

When You Arrive by Private Boat

Village and Dinner Bays

Village and Dinner bays, at Mayne Island's western end, are used by residents during summer for mooring boats. Both bays are exposed to winds and ferry wash from Trincomali Channel and are not good overnight anchorages. They can, however, be used temporarily if you want to walk around Village Bay or pick up someone arriving aboard a ferry.

Graveyard at Miners Bay.

Miners Bay

Miners Bay, midway through Active Pass, has a government wharf with space for half a dozen boats. All of the facilities in Miners Bay are right above the dock, and commercial outlets can provide supplies needed by boaters, including fuel and groceries.

Miners Bay is a busy community in summer and an interesting stopping point for walks around the village or along Georgina Point Road at the edge of the bay. Tides can be strong in the bay and the wharf is open to wash from the ferries.

David Cove

David Cove, on the north side of Mayne, is a safe anchorage to wait for the tide in Active Pass. It is small, surrounded by homes and exposed to north winds from Georgia Strait, but winds are not usually a problem here in summer. The walk from David Cove to Active Pass Light Station is less than three kilometres, and there is pleasant walking in the Edith Point area.

Campbell and Bennett Bays

Both Campbell and Bennett bays are exposed to southeasterlies but can be used as temporary anchorages. There's good beachcombing here and the work of local artists may be for sale not far from the beaches.

Horton Bay

Horton Bay is a safe anchorage with a government wharf and space for a few boats. The area is interesting to explore by dinghy, but currents in the channels around Curlew, Lizard and Samuel islands can run up to five knots, so watch the tides. The walk inland from Horton Bay toward Fernhill Road passes some beautiful farmland and woods.

Piggott and Gallagher Bays

These bays, on the south side of Mayne, offer the only anchorage on this side of the island, but they can be used only temporarily. Piggott Bay is dangerously exposed to southeast winds from Plumper Sound, and Gallagher Bay is shallow and spotted by reefs. The beach at Piggott Bay, however, is one of the nicest on Mayne Island.

Mayne Island Fishing — Action in Active Pass

Launching: at Village Bay to fish the southwest end, David Cove to fish the northeast end.

The paved launching ramp at David Cove is located on the east side of the cove. Drive along Waugh Road and slightly more than one kilometre from the start of the road, turn left on Porter Road. Almost immediately after turning onto Porter, turn left again on a short lane called Petrus Crescent. The ramp is at the end of the road. The Village Bay ramp is at the end of Callaghan Crescent off Mariners Way.

Active Pass fishing is renowned on the lower B.C. coast and plays a significant role in the economy of Mayne Island. There is a special section on Active Pass in Chapter 1, and methods of fishing Helen Point, Miners Bay, Gossip Island, Georgina Point and Georgina Shoals are described in the chapter on Galiano Island.

Navy Channel — Plumper Sound

Launching: Village Bay or Piggott Bay.

Navy Channel and Plumper Sound are not rated high by Gulf Island sport fishermen but there is some trolling for chinooks off St. John Point,

Sea lions, common near Helen Point.

150

at the southeast end of Mayne Island. Good-sized springs are occasionally caught along the southern shoreline between the point and Conconi Reef. The reef is a hot spot for cod.

Mayne Island Scuba Diving

Enterprise Reef

Boat dive — launching at Village Bay.

Enterprise Reef, half a mile off Crane Point near the southwest entrance to Active Pass, is near a busy waterway with swift currents and lots of bull kelp. It should be dived by experienced divers only, with someone in the boat at all times and diver identification clearly visible to other boaters.

The underwater scenery here is exceptionally beautiful, with bull kelp, scallops, ling cod and rockfish, abalone, sea stars and king crabs. White anemones cling to a sheer cliff on the south side of the reef which drops to about 30 metres. The north side is shallower, with interesting plants and animals at eight or nine metres.

Conconi Reef

Boat dive — launching at Village Bay or Piggott Bay.

Conconi Reef, in Navy Channel between Mayne and North Pender islands, is rocky with a variety of marine life at a depth of about 12 metres. There is a slight current at certain times, and it should be dived close to slack tide with a person on the surface in a boat.

Bennett Bay

Shore dive.

The rocks along the southeast end of Bennett Bay make for interesting diving at a depth of 10 or 12 metres. There are numerous anemones and sea stars, a few bottomfish and countless rock and hermit crabs. The beach is accessible by a public access lane off Wilkes Road in the Bennett Bay area.

Wreck of the *Zephyr*

Boat dive — launching at David Cove.

The wreck of the *Zephyr*, protected under the Heritage Conservation Act of B.C., lies just offshore in about 10 metres of water midway between David Cove and Edith Point. Discovered by divers in 1977, the *Zephyr* went down in 1872 while carrying sandstone blocks and columns from Newcastle Island to be used for construction of a mint in San Francisco.

Georgina Shoals

Boat dive — launching at David Cove.

Georgina Shoals, less than half a mile north of Active Pass Light Station, is among the finest dives in the Gulf Islands, with prolific marine life and kelp at a depth of about 10 metres. There is an interesting and intricate conglomeration of rocks and reefs, with abalone and bottomfish for gourmet divers.

Although not as busy as Enterprise Reef, Georgina Shoals see a fair amount of traffic, particularly sport fishermen in search of lunker salmon off Georgina Point on the shoals. Currents can be strong here, and someone should be on the surface in a boat with diver identification.

Active Pass

Boat or shore dive — launching at Village Bay or David Cove.

Virtually everywhere in Active Pass is good diving territory, but it is deep and dangerous due to currents and heavy marine traffic. There is a section on Active Pass diving in the chapter on Galiano Island.

After Mayne, What Next?

Mayne is a small island which can be toured in a few hours. It is easily accessible for day-trips from Tsawwassen and Swartz Bay at any time of week year-round. The leisurely pace is probably its most attractive feature. Like Galiano or Saturna, Mayne Island has many of the same characteristics as other outer Gulf Islands, yet possesses its own distinctive features. Determining which island is best for you is simply a matter of seeing them all.

Saturna

Outback of the Gulf Islands

 Saturna Island, the outback of the Gulf Islands, is the most remote and least populated of the islands served by B.C. ferries. With 31 square kilometres, it is larger than Mayne or either of the Penders but is inhabited by fewer than 350 people. Located at the easternmost end of the group, Saturna is a mountainous island with the second-highest peaks in the Gulf Islands. Five of the peaks rise above 300 metres and the highest, Mount Warburton Pike, looms 490 metres over Plumper Sound. The summit is the highest point on Saturna's "Brown Ridge," a steep and barren hillside on the south side of the island which is clearly visible from points on the Penders, Saltspring and Vancouver Island.

153

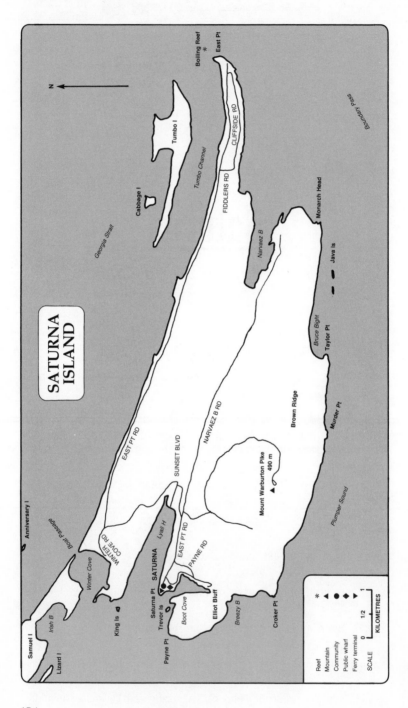

SATURNA ISLAND

Self-sufficiency is a way of life for Saturna Islanders, and most permanent residents are able to do a number of jobs rather than practise just one occupation. Electricians, fishermen, teachers, farmers and other workers are usually willing to take on odd jobs in other lines of work to help maintain the independent lifestyles they have chosen. While the island is too far from major centres for regular commuting, some Saturna Islanders occasionally work at projects on other islands for a few weeks at a time. Tourism is not a significant factor in Saturna Island's economy. Most visitors have friends or relatives who own property on the island or come only for day-trips. Much of the population is centred around Lyall Harbour and Boot Cove and a few homes are scattered throughout the island.

The island was named in 1791 after the Spanish naval schooner *Saturnina*, commanded by Captain Jose Maria Narvaez. The ship was part of the expedition that, in the same year, discovered Georgia Strait, which the Spaniards named *Gran Canal Nostra Senora del Rosario la Marinera*. The name was later changed to Georgia Strait by surveyors of the Royal Navy.

Captain George Henry Richards, who was commissioned in 1856 to the steam sloop *Plumper* to survey the coast, named and renamed many of the harbours, bays, channels, islands, points and other landmarks of the Gulf Islands, but he also retained a number of names already used by previous explorers. Richards arrived on this coast in 1857 but found the 484-tonne *Plumper* too small and unsuitable for his survey. It was replaced by the 860-tonne *Hecate* which Richards used until his return to England, with the *Hecate*, in 1863.

Winter Cove Park.

Richards's survey was continued until 1870 by Captain Daniel Pender, who came to the coast as second master aboard the *Plumper*. Pender finished the survey with the Hudson's Bay Company paddle steamer *Beaver*, the first steam vessel on the B.C. coast. The names of various features around Saturna Island are a combination of those given by the Spaniards, the British surveyors and early Gulf Island settlers.

Saturna Island is a day-tripper's island. Accommodation is scarce, public campgrounds are non-existent and access to much of the waterfront is limited. B.C. Ferry service from Tsawwassen, Swartz Bay and other islands varies with the days and seasons and should be carefully considered before planning a trip to Saturna.

If you can sort out the ferry schedules, Saturna is an interesting destination. There is no loop or circle route for a whirlwind tour, but a 35-kilometre drive or cycle around the main roads will take you to some pretty beaches and viewpoints. Paddlers and small boaters will find some fascinating water at the northwestern end, between Saturna and Mayne islands, and fishermen will enjoy some of the Gulf Islands' finest salmon fishing off East Point.

A Route to Follow

From the ferry terminal at Saturna Point, East Point Road runs along the southern side of Lyall Harbour to a valley at the head of the harbour. Stay to the left, passing roads to Boot Cove and Narvaez Bay, and descend into the valley. It is a sleepy-looking hollow with cottages and a small schoolhouse nestled between the wooded slopes of the harbour. Deer often graze on the school grounds and raccoons are a common sight in the surrounding forests.

There are glimpses of Lyall Harbour as East Point Road climbs out of the valley and eventually meets Winter Cove Road. A left turn takes you to Winter Cove, site of a 91-hectare provincial park purchased in 1979 for $500,000. The park, which has been provided with a loop-trail, outhouses, picnic tables, a boat ramp, fire pits and other day-use facilities, includes more than two kilometres of shoreline along the eastern side of the cove and around Winter Point to the north side of the island. The trail follows the shore to the point, passing two swamps, one surrounded by tall bulrushes.

Plans to develop the park for camping seem to have fallen through due to objections from island residents, who are worried about increased ferry traffic and fire hazards. Many of the islanders believe they should have priority over tourists on the ferries and feel it is the provincial government's responsibility to ensure they won't be stranded at terminals during the height of the tourist season. There are differing opinions on that topic, but it is hoped that some agreement over public use of the park can be reached. Winter Cove is one of the most beautiful parts of Saturna, and the park would provide a sorely needed camping spot for overnight visitors.

The park features stands of cedar and a few huge arbutus trees which hang over the beach from the top of a low-lying bank. Ducks and other migratory birds feed in the swamps and numerous other waterfowl winter in the cove. Blacktail deer, raccoons, mink and river otters leave their tracks

East Point foghorn.

on the beach, and harbour seals and sea lions come into the bay to feed. Winter Point is separated from Samuel Island by Boat Passage, which connects the cove with the waters of Georgia Strait. There is a grassy ledge on the point, an irresistible place to stretch out for a summer snooze. It would make a fine campsite.

The route from Winter Cove to East Point is a long and leisurely trip through forests of small firs, cedars, various deciduous trees and giant arbutus, some of which reach across the road toward the sea. The roadway is skirted by dense underbrush of salal, blackberry bushes, bracken and sword ferns.

Exactly one kilometre from the junction of Winter Cove and East Point roads, there is a narrow lane to the beach. It is a tiny gravel and shell beach with lots of driftwood. From here you can walk along the northern shore of Saturna for good views over Georgia Strait.

The road climbs gradually as it approaches East Point, providing good views of Tumbo Island and Channel. As it drops back to sea level, it passes a short sidestreet named Salal Road, a place worth stopping for a fine view up the northern shoreline of Saturna.

East Point Lighthouse was built in 1888 and remained under the care of the Georgeson family for more than half a century. The first lightkeeper served only one year before James Georgeson, who had come from the Shetland Islands to settle on the Gulf Islands, took charge. His wife was the first white woman to live on Saturna and their son was the first white child born on the island. Georgeson, whose name lives on in the Gulf Islands, is credited with being the main force behind a pension plan for lightkeepers. After he left East Point in 1924 he was succeeded by two of his sons.

East Point is every naturalist's dream, and trips to this most easterly point in the Gulf Island group should be planned to coincide with low tide. You can leave your car or bicycle outside the lighthouse gates and walk down a steep access to a shell and gravel beach facing Tumbo Island.

There are strange rock formations toward the point, where the never-ending motion of waves has eroded the sandstone over the centuries, carving deep into cliff faces to create smooth shelves and pools. The sandstone is mixed with lumpy conglomerate and the cracks and crevices around the point have become tidal pools, natural outdoor aquariums teeming with marine life — multi-coloured anemones, spiny spider crabs, limpets, mussels, barnacles, bullheads, hermit crabs, periwinkles, starfish and a host of others.

Kelp beds curl around the tip of the point and many species of diving birds poke around the kelp in search of deep-sea delicacies. There are several duck species — loons, grebes, cormorants, murres, guillemots, auklets and more. Bald eagles, oystercatchers and cormorants often stand on Boiling Reef, off the end of the point, while gulls and terns circle overhead, plucking minnows and small baitfish from the surface.

If you are lucky you will see a parasitic jaeger carrying out its piratical pursuit of a defenceless tern. A jaeger is a hawk-like seabird with falcon-shaped wings and elongated tail feathers. It earns a living by swooping down on a feeding tern and forcing the tern to drop its baitfish so the jaeger can snatch it up for itself. The attack and ensuing chase are inevitably accompanied by frantic squeals and general commotion throughout the whole bird community.

The baitfish which attract the birds also lure salmon that school up in back eddies around the point. Salmon is a favourite dish for harbour seals, northern sea lions and killer whales. While seals and sea lions are still fairly common in the islands, whale sightings are slowly becoming a rare treat. East Point is regarded as one of the best places in the Gulf Islands to watch for the whales, especially during summer.

An entire day can easily be spent at East Point, on the sandstone shores facing Boiling Reef or lolling around the beach. You can climb up the edge of the point and look across neatly manicured lawns to the lighthouse or visit the lighthouse during certain hours.

At East Point, if you're facing the lighthouse, there's a parking area and public access on the left that leads to a beach overlooking Tumbo Channel. Another trail which follows the lighthouse fence is private property and out of bounds to the public. At low tides you can walk along the shore to the end of the point for a look at more marine and bird life and good views of the American San Juan Islands. Freighters heading in and out of Georgia and Juan de Fuca straits use the route around East Point.

When you leave the lighthouse and head back toward Winter Cove, you can turn left onto Cliffside Road, which follows the southern side of East Point to Fiddlers Cove. Part of this area is a wildlife sanctuary, established to preserve the habitat for birds and mammals that thrive at East Point. Fiddlers Road returns to East Point Road and takes you back toward the ferry terminal.

What the Main Route Misses

Lyall Harbour Beach

Sunset Boulevard, in the valley at the head of Lyall Harbour, divides the valley and ends at a gravel beach which faces across Plumper Sound to Navy Channel, between Mayne and North Pender islands. It is one of the few accessible beaches on Saturna and a good spot for a picnic or a dip in the frigid waters of the bay. Ferries approaching the terminal from Plumper Sound can be seen from this beach, so you could wait for a ferry here and have enough time to reach the terminal between the time you see it and the time it docks.

Narvaez Bay

About 1.5 kilometres from the ferry terminal, Narvaez Bay Road forks to the right off East Point Road. Narvaez Bay is approximately eight kilometres from this intersection, but there is no marked public access from the road to the water. The drive is a bit rough but the scenery is nice, with wooded hillsides, a small local cemetery and a few comfortable-looking cabins. Any spot along Narvaez Bay Road is a good place to walk, and your chances of seeing deer are good.

Boot Cove

Boot Cove and Payne roads run down to the right off East Point Road a short distance from the ferry terminal, and while there are no marked accesses to the cove, a drive around these roads provides an interesting look at some of the homes and properties of Saturna Island's main population centre.

Transportation

Lyall Harbour is the terminus for all B.C. ferries to Saturna Island. Check local businesses for information on airline and water taxi services.

Boot Cove.

Emergencies and Information

On Saturna Island call 911 in case of an emergency. RCMP on the Pender Islands are responsible for law enforcement on Saturna.

Local businesses and islanders can provide information on just about anything on Saturna Island.

Camping and Accommodation

There are no public campgrounds on Saturna. For up-to-date listings of private campgrounds, lodges, cottages, bed-and-breakfast establishments or other accommodation, check Tourism B.C.'s *Accommodations* booklet, described in Chapter 1.

Shopping and Services

Saturna is serviced by a small number of stores, a liquor outlet, pub and fuel station.

Recreation and Events

There are tennis courts open to the public on Saturna. Islanders can provide information on fishing, cruising and other activities.

The Saturna Island Canada Day lamb bake traditionally has been held on the July 1 weekend since 1949.

Saturna Island Hiking —
Mountain Climbing, Seaside Strolling

Mount Warburton Pike

Mount Warburton Pike, at 490 metres the highest peak on Saturna, is accessible by a winding gravel road that is suitable for most cars but is more enjoyable as a hiking route. It can be reached by turning onto Narvaez Bay Road from East Point Road and turning left on Harris Road, across from Saturna General Store. Follow Harris less than half a kilometre to a hairpin bend up to the left. The summit is almost four kilometres up from this turn, and though the road is steep and lumpy in places, it can be driven by cautious drivers.

Mount Warburton Pike is named in honour of one of the Gulf Islands' most remarkable pioneers, an Englishman who dropped his studies at Oxford to seek a life of adventure in North America. Warburton Pike arrived on Saturna Island after canoeing down the Yukon River in 1892 and '93. He had gone to the Northwest Territories in search of musk-ox and wrote a book about his experiences in the north in 1892. He and a friend, another Englishman named Charles Payne, bought a farm on Saturna for $5,000 in 1884 and later started a stone quarry on Plumper Sound.

The road to the top of the mountain passes a 131-hectare ecological reserve, set aside to preserve a typical west coast Douglas fir forest. There is some radio and television equipment at the top which should not be touched.

Feral goats, descendants of domestic animals gone wild at the turn of the century, roam the slopes of Mount Warburton Pike. They are shy of human intruders but you may see some. The summit can be an eerie place on breezy winter days when a gray mist settles over the hillsides. Ravens linger in the updrafts at eye-level, like vultures hovering over a carcass, and the only sounds are the wind in the treetops and the ravens' ghoulish cries.

On the seashore at the foot of the ridge, southeast of the mountain peak, is Murder Point, so named after a gruesome double slaying which

A frequent Saturna sight.

led to the destruction of an entire Indian village. A man named Frederick Marks, who had been living with his family on nearby Waldron Island in the American San Juans, decided to move to Mayne Island in November of 1862. The family and their belongings were travelling in two boats when they were separated by inclement weather in Plumper Sound.

Marks and a daughter landed on Saturna's south shore between Murder and Croker Points. While lighting a fire, Marks was shot by Indians. His daughter fled and the remains of her naked body were found several months later, stuffed into a crevice and covered by boulders.

News of the savagery didn't reach Victoria until the following April, but as it was the policy of the colonial government to spare no expense in punishing murderers of white people, four ships were dispatched to search the coast and apprehend the killers. The search culminated in a ruthless attack on a Lamalchi Indian village at Kuper Island. Several Indians and one white man were killed in the raid, and the village was obliterated. Eleven men and six women were arrested and four of the men were hanged in July 1863.

Above Murder Point, the south slope of Mount Warburton Pike is steep, with evergreens clinging to the hillside all the way to the bottom. There are excellent views of the Penders, other Gulf Islands, Vancouver Island and the San Juans. This mountain looks similar to Mount Tuam on Saltspring Island.

Saturna's Unhurried Roads

Nearly all of the roads on Saturna make good hiking routes because traffic, even in summer, is generally light. East Point Road, between the turnoff to Winter Cove and East Point, is one of the nicest roads for walking because it follows the shore of Georgia Strait and the ocean is visible for much of the hike. A five-kilometre trek around a loop from East Point along Cliffside Road to Fiddlers Road, then back to East Point, is an easy two-hour stroll.

Canoeing and Small Boating — Sheltered Seas and Open Waters

Winter Cove to Mayne Island

Distance: nine nautical miles. *Launching:* Winter Cove.

The launching area at Winter cove is not paved and can be used by trailer boats only under appropriate tidal conditions. The ground is fairly hard and a half tide is necessary to avoid getting stuck.

163

Winter Cove is a starting point for a small-boat trip through a fascinating maze of islands and channels between Saturna and Mayne islands. If you launch from the parking area at the head of the cove, you can take a cruise around the islands between Winter Cove and Bennett Bay on Mayne. You will see some neat waterfront cabins, and horses grazing, near the shore of Samuel Island if you travel along the southern side toward Irish Bay. Hug the shoreline beyond the bay and into Georgeson Passage between Samuel and Lizard islands. The water is shallow in the channel and tides can run up to five knots and flip a canoe or kayak at full flood. Currents all around this end of Samuel, Curlew and Lizard islands can be dangerous to small boats and are best travelled as close as possible to slack tide.

Georgeson Passage continues on between Samuel and Curlew islands and into Bennett Bay, on Mayne Island. You can travel back across Horton Bay and through the channels on the south sides of Curlew and Lizard islands toward Winter Cove. If you follow the southern side of Winter Cove back to the launching area, you will pass Church Cove, site of St. Christopher's Church. The building, no longer in use, was converted from a Japanese boathouse around the turn of the century.

WINTER COVE AREA

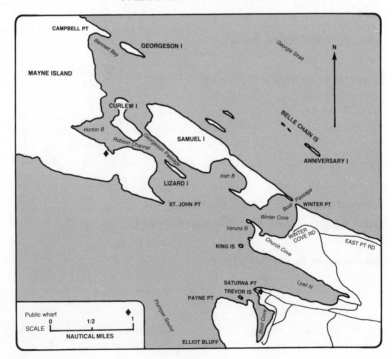

Winter Cove to Belle Chain Islets

Distance: four nautical miles. *Launching:* Winter Cove.

Winter Cove is also a launching point for another small boat or canoe trip through Boat Passage to nearby islets in Georgia Strait. Extreme caution should be exercised when moving through Boat Passage, as it narrows to about 15 metres, causing tides to rip through at seven knots.

Church Cove.

165

If you can't wait for slack tide, a small craft can be portaged over the tip of Winter Point with a bit of grunting.

Due north of the passage is a group of islets known as the Belle Chain, site of a shipwreck which occurred during a snowstorm in 1916. The Japanese vessel *Ken Kon Maru*, loaded with barbed wire and railway ties, was bound for Russia when she piled up on the reefs near Anniversary Island. Despite the bad weather the crew made it safely ashore. Six months later the vessel was salvaged.

There's more interesting exploring near the Belle Chain Islets, around two islets off the north shore of Samuel Island. Raccoons are occasionally seen here foraging along the sea shore.

Cabbage Island

Distance: six nautical miles. *Launching:* small lane off East Point Road one kilometre from intersection at Winter Cove Road, or at Winter Cove.

Cabbage Island, a long-time favourite anchorage for yachtsmen, is a four-hectare marine park off the northwest end of Tumbo Island. It was purchased in 1978 through the co-operation of the Nature Conservancy of Canada and the Devonian Foundation of Alberta, two private organizations dedicated to the preservation of valuable recreational lands. It has been developed as a marine park by the Provincial Parks Branch.

There is no water on the island and camping facilities are minimal, but Cabbage is known for its beautiful sandy beaches and grassy uplands. There are two good camping beaches on the south side.

The journey from the launching spot to Cabbage Island is about three miles. Tidal streams, which reach five knots off East Point, increase in velocity as you approach Tumbo Channel. An unusual characteristic of tides in Tumbo Channel is that they flow to the east on both the ebb and flood. This abnormal flow is caused by an enormous back eddy which coils around the tip of East Point and over the end of Tumbo Island. These currents explain why salmon fishing off East Point is among the hottest in the Gulf Islands. People in naturally powered craft should be wary of tides when crossing the channel, as you could get swept into the rips off East Point.

Boot Cove

Distance: 1.5 nautical miles. *Launching:* government wharf at Lyall Harbour.

Boot Cove can be deceptively calm, and although it appears to be a sheltered enclave it is not. Winter winds funnel into the cove between the steep sides, occasionally ripping boats from their moorings and docks from their pilings. Wharf repairs in Boot Cove are an annual chore for property owners along the shores.

You can tour the cove and circumnavigate Trevor Islet before returning to the wharf. If the weather is good, you could take a cruise around Lyall Harbour and into Winter Cove, or go the other direction, around Payne Point and across Breezy Bay to Croker Point.

Boot Cove.

When You Arrive by Private Boat

Lyall Harbour

Lyall Harbour is the site of a government wharf. Fuel and a store to provide for boaters is within walking distance. Nearby Boot Cove can be used as an overnight anchorage in calm weather, but the land around the cove is privately owned and there is little access to shore.

Breezy Bay

Breezy Bay is sheltered from southeast winds and is a good place to drop anchor on a summer evening.

Saturna's Eastern End

Bruce Bight, Narvaez Bay and Fiddlers Cove provide temporary moorage at Saturna's eastern end, but the shorelines are steep and there are no particularly good places to walk. They are pleasant places to moor if you are looking for some privacy, but they are exposed to the southeast.

Winter Cove

Winter Cove, site of a 91-hectare provincial park, is a secluded corner of Saturna which is protected from all but northwest winds. It is fairly shallow and the western entrance is partially blocked by reefs, but the cove is one of the nicest anchorages on Saturna Island. It can be entered from Georgia Strait through Boat Passage, an extremely narrow channel where tides flow up to seven knots.

Saturna Island Fishing — Salmon and Cutthroat Trout

East Point

Launching: Winter Cove or Lyall Harbour.

Winter Cove and Lyall Harbour are the only launching areas on Saturna, although a small boat could be carried down a lane to the beach on the north side of East Point near the lighthouse. The Winter Cove and Lyall Harbour launches are not paved and can be used for trailer boats only under appropriate tidal conditions. A full tide is needed to launch at Lyall Harbour because of soft ground, and Winter Cove, with a slightly harder surface, can be used on a half tide.

East Point is one of the best Gulf Island fishing grounds and is fished throughout the summer by anglers from both sides of Georgia Strait. An enormous back eddy forms off the end of the point and swirls all the way around the eastern end of Tumbo Island. It is a favourite spot for drift fishing, mooching and trolling. Killer whales are often seen by fishermen off East Point.

Lyall Harbour

Launching: at head of Lyall Harbour.

Good-sized springs and cohoes often pass Saturna Point and linger off the mouth of Lyall Harbour at certain times of year. You can troll in these areas, drift fish or cast from the government wharf. Spincasters tossing lures off the wharf while waiting for ferries have been known to land lunker salmon.

Lyall Harbour is also known for its sea-run cutthroat fishing off the mouth of Lyall Creek. Cutthroat to four pounds are occasionally caught by fly fishermen and spincasters in the shallows at the head of the bay. Fish a flood tide in early morning or at dusk.

Saturna Island Scuba Diving

Elliot Bluff

Boat dive — launching at head of Lyall Harbour.

Elliot Bluff, at the southwest end of Saturna, is a sheer cliff where some of the Gulf Islands' largest sea anemones cling to rock walls plunging to the depths. The anemone show begins only a few metres from the surface and continues down the side of the bluff for about 30 metres. There are lots of big fish here and a slight current.

Java Islets

Boat dive — launching at Lyall Harbour.

Java Islets, near Saturna's southeast end, make one of the Gulf Islands' nicer dives, with kelp beds, abalone and urchins dominating the scenery.

The best sights are at about 10 or 12 metres and the depth drops sharply on either side of the islets.

Taylor Point

Boat dive — launching at Lyall Harbour.

Taylor Point, less than a mile west of Java Islets, is known for its old bottles and junk which must have been dumped from a wharf, the remains of which are still underwater here. The scenery, including some large, old iron beams, is at a depth of about nine metres. Taylor Point and Java Islets can be explored in one day.

After Saturna, What Next?

Saturna is remote and not easily accessible by comparison to the other Gulf Islands and, because of this, it is an island which is not likely to change dramatically in the foreseeable future. After touring Saturna it is interesting to visit a more populated island, such as Saltspring, and see the differences in lifestyles from one island to another. The pace on Saltspring is fast, by Saturna standards, yet Saltspring is often regarded by outsiders as a salty holm for contented laggards. It simply proves that no two islands are entirely alike.

Gulf Islands Marine Parks

For Paddlers, Cruisers and Sailors

 In British Columbia there are more than 250,000 families

who own boats. Undoubtedly those who live near the Gulf

Islands are the most fortunate, for it's here, where winter temperatures

infrequently dip below freezing, that boating is truly a year-round pastime.

More than 100,000 Canadian boats are based on and around the waters

of Georgia Strait, and about 25,000 American pleasure boaters travel in

the Gulf Islands each year. Studies show that throughout the Capital Region,

which encompasses Greater Victoria and the southern Gulf Islands, one

family in five owns at least one boat: pleasure boating is believed to be

the single most popular recreational pastime in the region.

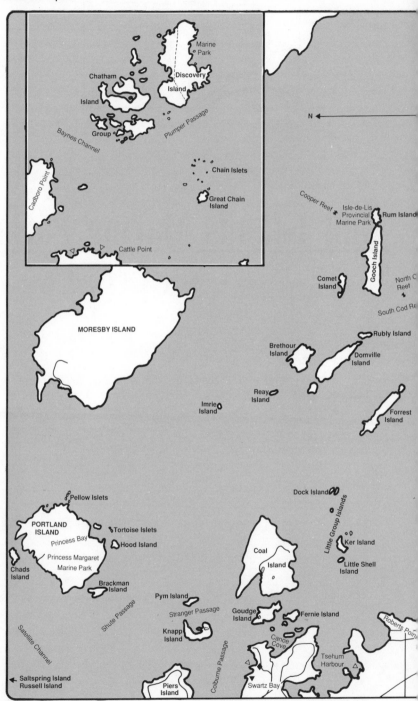

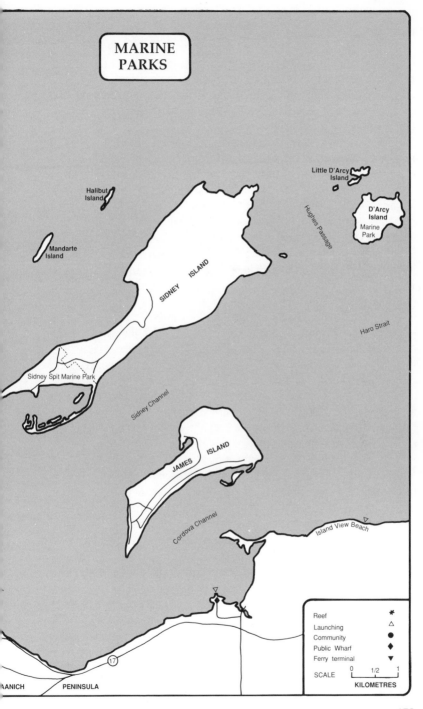

MARINE
PARKS

Little D'Arcy
Island

D'Arcy
Island
Marine
Park

Halibut
Island

Hughes Passage

Mandarte
Island

SIDNEY ISLAND

Haro Strait

Sidney Spit Marine Park

Sidney Channel

ISLAND

JAMES ISLAND

Cordova Channel

Island View Beach

Reef	✳
Launching	△
Community	●
Public Wharf	◆
Ferry terminal	▼

SCALE 0   1/2   1

KILOMETRES

AANICH   PENINSULA

(17)

To preserve public space for these vacationing mariners, in 1959 the provincial government established Montague Harbour Provincial Marine Park, the first of its kind in B.C. The marine parks system has grown with the boating fraternity and now there are more than 30 marine parks in B.C., most of them in southern waters. Some of these parks — Montague on Galiano, Beaumont on South Pender, Winter Cove on Saturna, and Cabbage Island, a few strokes off Saturna's northeast shores — are described in previous chapters.

The most noticeable change among B.C. boaters in recent years is a marked proliferation of kayakers. When the first edition of *The Gulf Islands Explorer* was published in 1981, kayakers in the Gulf Islands were a rare sight. Nearly a decade later, when this revised edition was produced, it seemed the Gulf Islands had become a kayakers' mecca. It is estimated now that as many as 3,000 kayakers a year may tour parts of the Gulf Islands. It's because of the phenomenal interest in kayaking the Gulf Islands that this new chapter on marine parks of the southern islands was added. With the addition of Portland, Sidney, D'Arcy, Rum and Discovery islands, *The Gulf Islands Explorer* now covers all marine parks in the southern Gulf Islands.

On the 23 separate canoe trips described in previous chapters, the safety of shore is always within easy reach. But all of the marine parks described in this chapter lie farther offshore. Kayakers travelling to these islands should be experienced or should paddle with seasoned kayakers. Sidney and Portland islands could be reached in open canoes, but canoeing to Rum, D'Arcy and Discovery Islands should be attempted only when you're assured of good weather. Recorded marine weather forecasts, which are updated throughout the day, are available by calling telephone numbers under federal government listings.

Although summer days are warmer and longer, they are not necessarily calmer. During winter there are often several consecutive days when ripples rarely appear on the surface of the sea. The ocean is motionless, like an endless mirror, an irresistible invitation to anyone who's enjoyed the comfort, the confidence, and the rhythm of paddling to a distant destination. Winter is also the time for wildlife: the sea lions are here in winter and there are literally tens of thousands of seabirds.

Information on basic equipment, charts, tide tables and other requirements for Gulf Islands paddlers appears in the small boating section of Chapter 1. For winter paddlers, it is also a good idea to carry a package of signal flares and, if space allows, a change of clothes, especially if small children are among the group. If you get dumped in winter it is much more difficult than in summer to get dry and warm, so a section on dealing with hypothermia has been included in this chapter. Hazards, suggested routes, launching points, and highlights along the way to each island are also covered.

Hypothermia — The Chill That Kills

Hypothermia is a widely misunderstood, often ignored phenomenon that claims dozens of lives every year. In the cold waters of the Gulf Islands it can snuff out a life within a couple of hours.

Simply defined, hypothermia is a lowering of the inner body temperature, causing severely reduced blood circulation and profound impairment of normal body functions. A wet boater will begin to lose heat from the skin, or peripheral tissues, almost immediately. It takes 10 or 15 minutes, however, before the heart and brain begin to cool.

The first reaction is to shiver. Shivering is a chemical increase in energy production that raises the warmth level by approximately five times: it should never be suppressed. But in cold water — which in the Gulf Islands could vary from a winter low of about 4 degrees Celsius to perhaps 15 or 16 in summer — shivering is an inadequate form of heat production. An average 70-kilogram person will lose consciousness within about an hour and a half of the dunking, when the inner body temperature drops from the normal 37 degrees to between 30 and 32 degrees. The temperature falls to about 24 degrees during the next hour, the heart fibrillates, and the misery ends. Some people, of course, live longer than others in cold water. A small child, in water of 10 degrees, could be dead within an hour, while an obese person may last up to six hours because of insulative blubber.

Getting dumped from a boat isn't the only way to contract hypothermia. Simply getting damp from rain or ocean spray can be enough. The symptoms of hypothermia are not always obvious. A person in the early stages may not acknowledge a problem and deny having any ill feeling. He shivers and feels numb, but may appear of sound mind, having no appreciation for the seriousness of his condition. A few moments later the shivering intensifies; it's out of control. By the time he begins to ramble incoherently, his mind is sluggish. His physical co-ordination fails and he stumbles. He is no longer able to care for himself.

Members of an outdoor group should constantly watch each other, particularly in damp, cold weather. A general rule is to believe the symptoms, not the victim, when hypothermia is apparently taking hold.

Exercise, when possible, will help a hypothermic hiker produce body heat, but in cold water the opposite is the case. Someone who tries to swim ashore from an overturned boat cools 35 per cent faster than a person who floats motionless in a life jacket. A position known as the "heat escape lessening posture (HELP)" helps retain warmth in high heat-loss areas such as the groin, neck and sides of the chest. A hypothermia victim, either floating in a life jacket or sitting on land, simply holds the arms tight against the chest sides and pulls the knees up, to reduce the flow of cold air or water over the crucial areas.

In situations where the victim needs assistance, the most important thing is to remove wet clothing. The primary cause of air hypothermia is dampness. If wet clothing is cooled by air or wind, hypothermia strikes quickly.

Here are some basic treatments for hypothermia:

- Place the victim, stripped, in a sleeping bag with one, preferably two, warm people, also stripped. Skin-to-skin contact is one of the most effective rewarming methods.
- Rescuers should breathe close to the mouth and nostrils of the victim, providing warmth to the core of the body through inhalation. When possible, water should be boiled and steam directed under a makeshift hood over the hypothermic person's head.
- Apply hot, wet towels or blankets.
- Give hot, nonalcoholic drinks.
- Don't move the hypothermic person until he or she is sufficiently rewarmed. Then pack up the planned activities and go home. Never continue the trip.

Both air and water hypothermia can be worsened by complications such as injury or dehydration, but usually they can be avoided by a basic understanding of the causes. Before an outdoors excursion, it should be determined which members of the group are most susceptible and they should be watched most closely. Boaters should be aware of available survival equipment, such as the UVic Thermofloat jacket, a coat which provides buoyancy and helps retain body heat. Other cold-water survival suits are also available.

Hypothermia is slowly becoming a household word in North America. But in spite of exhaustive research, the widespread ignorance concerning this insidious assassin of outdoors enthusiasts remains clearly evident. Coroner's juries continue to rule "death by drowning" when all indications point toward hypothermia, or hypothermia-induced drowning, as the killer in many cases. Even more disturbing is the inane it-can't-happen-to-me attitude. It can happen to anyone.

Portland Island — An Island for a Princess

Launching: Tsehum Harbour; government wharf near Swartz Bay. *Hazards:* ferries and ferry wash. *Drinking water:* from a well.

Portland Island, 3.4 nautical miles northeast of Tsehum Harbour in Sidney, is a 194-hectare park. The island, originally owned by the Hudson's Bay Company, was eventually acquired by the province and given to Princess

Margaret in 1958 as a B.C. centennial gift. The princess returned it to the province, apparently with some reluctance, and in 1967 it was named Princess Margaret Provincial Marine Park in her honour. It is accessible only by boat and there are excellent beaches and grass fields for camping.

From Tsehum Harbour, paddle around Curteis Point through Page Pass, keeping an eye on swift-flowing tides, toward a marker off the north end of Goudge Island. Look for seals hauled out on rocks outside Canoe Cove. Fishing for cod can be good around the kelp beds and islets in the pass. Ferries from Swartz Bay travel in Colburne Passage, but most can be avoided by crossing the channel from Goudge Island, and heading for Stranger Pass, between Knapp and Pym islands. There's an open, one-mile stretch across Shute Passage to Portland Island: wind and wash from ferries and boats are the main dangers here.

One of the nicest campsites for paddlers is along Portland's southwest side. Piles of sun-bleached driftwood logs are scattered over the upper part of a pretty shell beach. Gently rolling grassland lies above the beach, with open campsites between big trees. Ferries run through Satellite Channel, on the island's north side, sending huge waves crashing to shore near Kanaka Bluff, named for Hawaiians who settled there in the 1800s. Ferry wash makes these waters an unsafe anchorage for large boats, leaving them for people with boats that can be pulled high and dry.

One of the beaches here is partially protected by Brackman Island, a five-hectare provincial ecological reserve established in 1989. The island is covered by Douglas fir — some 250 years old — arbutus, Garry oak, Rocky Mountain juniper and wildflowers.

Kayaks beached at Portland Island.

A three-mile circumnavigation of Portland Island passes beaches, sandstone shores, small islands and islets, reefs for bottomfishing, and good campsites. Princess Bay, west of Kanaka Bluff is "downtown" Portland Island. It's a well-sheltered anchorage, popular among boaters from Saanich Peninsula. There may be eagles nesting on Hood Island, just outside Princess Bay. A lovely sand and gravel beach curves along the head of the bay. Open fields above the beach provide the main campsite on the island, with outhouses and directional signs for island explorers.

Pellow Islets, on the east side of Portland, are good cod-fishing grounds and seals haul out on reefs here at low tide. There are lots of kelp beds, rocks and reefs which make these waters treacherous for cruisers and sailboats, intriguing for paddlers and divers. Beaches on this end of the island are small but secluded: some have reasonably private campsites above them.

Royal Cove, behind Chads Island, is another anchorage, but there are no beaches or campsites. Cod jigging off Chads Island can be productive.

Directional signs show a network of trails totalling about seven kilometres. One path leads to a hand pump for water, one cuts across the interior of the island between the two main anchorages, and another runs around the entire perimeter of the island. Apples can be picked in autumn from an old orchard above Princess Cove. A trail behind the orchard leads to some enormous ant hills.

Portland Island can also be reached from Fulford Harbour on Saltspring Island. This trip, however, is for experienced paddlers only, as it involves a crossing of 1.5 miles in open water over a major ferry route. You can launch at Drummond Park or Fulford government wharf and paddle along the shore for nearly 1.5 miles to Jackson Rock. From there it's slightly more than half a mile to Russell Island, on the Saltspring side of Satellite Channel. The open stretch across Satellite Channel to Portland Island is the main route for B.C. ferries steaming in and out of Swartz Bay. The trick is to get across the channel between ferries, without taking on water from ferry wash. If possible, the crossing should be made shortly after dawn, before there's an abundance of ferries using the channel. The crossing can be reduced by almost half a mile by paddling from Jackson Rock, east to Eleanor Point, then scooting across to Chads Island, near Portland Island. Eleanor Point can also be reached from Ruckle Park on Beaver Point.

Portland Island, because of its easy accessibility from Saanich Peninsula, is widely used by canoe and kayak clubs, youth and school groups. Once used to raise race horses, a few remnants of earlier days remain, but most of the island has gone wild. It's a great weekend destination.

Sidney Island — Wildlife and Sandy Shores

Launching: boat ramp at Tulista Park in Sidney; government wharf in downtown Sidney; Tsehum Harbour. *Hazards:* choppy seas generated by extremely heavy boat traffic; tides to three knots off Sidney Spit. *Drinking water:* from taps in Sidney Spit Provincial Marine Park.

The endless sandy beaches embellishing the shores of Sidney Island and nearby James Island are unique in the Gulf Islands. Nearly all of Sidney Island's 24 kilometres of shoreline are sand. Within the 400-hectare Sidney Spit Provincial Marine Park, there are two long, sandy spits, a shallow lagoon with an islet, forests and open grasslands. Only two nautical miles from the town of Sidney, the park is a favourite year-round beachcombing and bumming area for Saanich Peninsula boaters. In 1986 a private company, under contract to the provincial government, began running a summer foot-passenger ferry to the island from downtown Sidney. If there's room, you can pack a canoe or kayak aboard and avoid the often treacherous crossing from Sidney.

Sidney Channel, between Sidney and James islands, is the main route for commercial fishboats and other vessels steaming in and out of Haro Strait, which runs past Victoria to Juan de Fuca Strait. These boats, along with a multitude of yachts, runabouts, skiffs and ferries, put a constant chop on the channel: it can be uncomfortable paddling for nervous

Sidney Spit.

179

neophytes. Almost a full mile can be cut from the open water by paddling point-to-point along a 3.2-mile course from downtown Sidney. Paddle north to Roberts Point, then northeast to the Little Group Islands. From these islands it's a straight 1.1-mile shot across to the tip of Sidney Spit. Watch for fast tides off the spit.

It's little wonder Sidney Spit Park sees well over 60,000 visitors a year. More than half of the park's 400 hectares lie under the sea. Its main feature — a two-kilometre-long sand spit stabilized by log pilings — juts into the ocean from the north end of the island. Fishermen can spin-cast for salmon off the end of the spit in summer. Another equally long spit reaches along the western side of the island, forming a lagoon where Dungeness crabs wander through acres of eelgrass. The sandy shores on both sides of these spits are endless.

The entire island totals 916 hectares and most is privately owned. But the beaches are public, and those both inside and outside the park are spectacular. During low tides hundreds of hectares of open sand are exposed, leaving large shallow pools, perfect poking puddles for young explorers. Steamy veils of vapour rise from the beach as the summer sun beats down on the sand. Water coming in over the hot sand warms, at least for a short while, to reasonable swimming temperatures.

Although Sidney Island may not be a place for solitude, it is a paradise for naturalists. Among its 150-odd bird species are bald eagles, peregrine falcons, turkey vultures, ospreys and three types of hawks. There are three species of loons, three species of grebes and three species of cormorants. As many as 1,000 Brant use the lagoon during spring migrations, rhinoceros auklets are numerous in summer, and oldsquaw, black scoters, and Heermann's gulls pass through in fall. Marbled murrelets, western screech owls, purple martins and others occur naturally. There are also introduced species, including Reeve's pheasants, wild turkeys and common peafowl. Particularly noticeable in the park are great blue herons. More than 120 pairs nest near the head of the lagoon and forage in the shallows on both sides of the spit. Sidney Island is a predatorless haven for deer. There are literally hundreds of fallow deer on Sidney Island, a species introduced to James Island in the early 1900s. It's believed some fallow deer from James Island swam across Sidney Channel, probably in the 1950s, and established themselves on Sidney Island. Now visitors often see them lying under the shade of big Garry oak trees in fields above the lagoon. Groups of tawny does with spotted fawns lie in the bush, away from small bands of bucks. The biggest bucks are a velvet gray with impressive palmate antlers. If the deer are not lying in the fields, keen observers may see them just inside the edge of the forest where it meets the meadows. Blacktail deer, B.C. natives which were introduced to the island, are not as plentiful and are more commonly seen in the forests.

The forests and shores are also inhabited by mink, river otters, red squirrels, European rabbits, chipmunks, silver-haired bats and little brown bats. Bats have been known to spend daylight hours under the roof of an outdoor cooking shelter in the park's group camping area. Boaters and beachcombers at Sidney Island also may see killer whales, porpoises, harbour seals and California sea lions.

A short walk behind a private dock on the lagoon, there's a pond that's loaded with tree frogs in summer. About the size of a thumbnail, these little amphibians are the source of endless entertainment for young hunters who watch them climb the insides of glass jars with their sticky feet. They should be released within an hour, leaving them for the next group of hunters. These same frogs serenade campers to sleep.

An extensive network of trails and roads covers the park and, besides a group camping area, there are 12 developed and 50 undeveloped campsites.

As fascinating as Sidney Island's natural features is its history. Known as "Sallas" by Coast Salish Indians, it was used by natives of Saanich Peninsula as a place to collect crabs and clams. It became Hudson's Bay Company property, and when the company put it on the auction block in 1860, for six shillings an acre, there were no takers. Without protection from Indians, the settlers said, the island was worthless.

In 1902 George Courtenay of Victoria bought the entire island for $25,000. Between 1906 and 1915, Courtenay farmed the island, cut timber for railway ties, and in 1906 established the Sidney Island Tile and Brick Company. About 70 men, mainly Chinese, were employed to produced 55,000 bricks a year. A group of ten Victoria businessmen formed the

Campers on Sidney Island.

Sidney Island Syndicate in 1909 and purchased all but the 80-hectare Brick and Tile Company land for $150,000. The provincial government bought the remaining land in 1925; it was later expanded and Sidney Spit Marine Park was officially established in 1961. The rest of the island was owned by a variety of people over the years, but eventually the Todd family, of Victoria, acquired controlling interest. It was Jack Todd, a great nature lover and admirer of natural beauty, who was responsible for most of the island's development. He cleared roads and trails, built a cottage, barns and sheds, and operated a sheep farm to provide wool for Vancouver Island's Cowichan Indians. He dug several ponds to attract wildlife, then introduced peacocks, wild turkeys, bullfrogs and other animals.

In 1981, after a public furor over the government's refusal to accept Todd's offer to sell the island, it was bought by the Sallas Forest Limited Partnership. Much of the island was logged and replanted.

Remnants in the park of Sidney Island's human history include three archaeological sites, piles of broken bricks and decaying brick buildings, an old farmhouse and shed, and a moss-covered bomb shelter with benches inside.

Rum Island — Island of Lilies

Launching: boat ramp at Tulista Park in Sidney; government wharf in downtown Sidney; Tsehum Harbour. *Hazards:* heavy boat traffic; three-knot tides off Sidney Spit; strong southeast winds from Haro Strait. *Drinking water:* not available.

Rum Island, site of Isle-de-Lis Provincial Marine Park, is actually an isthmus on the east end of Gooch Island. Located 4.6 nautical miles due east of Sidney, all of this five-hectare island is parkland. It belongs to the people of B.C. through the generosity of Mrs. Renee Maccaud Nelson of White Rock, who bequeathed it to the province when she died in 1978. She loved wildflowers and asked that the park be named Isle-de-Lis.

With strong tides, winds and boat traffic, this trip is safest with a group and could be dangerous in open canoes. To minimize wide crossings, and take in as much scenery as possible, there's a six-mile course, hopping island-to-island, from Sidney. Paddle north to Roberts Point, then northeast past Little Shell and Ker islands to Dock Island. Paddle across the channel between Dock and the northwest end of Forrest Island, watching for strong tides and large boats. There's good cod fishing off this end of Forrest, and a two-mile circumnavigation of the island runs through several narrow channels, past islets and reefs. The island is privately owned but there are some pleasant beaches. The northeastern side of Forrest Island is the most scenic, so paddle to the other end of the island, then cross over to Domville Island. Run through the channel between Domville and Rubly islands, then head east to Gooch Island. The shorelines between Gooch and Comet islands, and along the north side of Gooch, are quite striking.

North Cod and South Cod reefs, off the southwest side of Gooch Island, are well known by scuba divers and, as the names imply, are good cod-fishing spots. Cooper Reef, north of Rum Island, and a reef with a marker off the east end of Rum are also good cod-fishing rocks.

Rum Island is a real gem, used little by yachtsmen because of poor anchorage. A tiny, two-sided beach joins the island to Gooch Island, but

Sculpted sandstone on Rum Island.

most of the shoreline is rocky, with numerous deep pockets cut into the shores. It's really a day-tripper's island, although there are some rough camping spots. Among the profusion of wildflowers which adorns the hillsides are Easter lilies and bright yellow stonecrop. The island is a wonderful place to while away a summer afternoon, and the journey to it, if you're cautious, is a fascinating paddle.

Rum Island lies only three-quarters of a mile from the Canada-U.S. border and was used during the days of prohibition as a stash for rum runners.

Mandarte Island, which from a distance appears as a rocky, whitewashed hump, is about 1.5 miles south of Rum Island. If weather is calm it's an interesting stop, but the crossing is wide open to winds in Haro Strait, which can catch you in mid-channel with little warning. A reef off the southeast end of Mandarte is a good cod spot and provides excellent snorkelling at extremely low tides.

Mandarte Island is a major bird-nesting island and an Indian reserve: permission is needed to land. There's really no need to go ashore, however, because the best views of nesting cormorants are from the water, at the base of high cliffs on the southwest side of Mandarte. During summer, about 900 pairs of double-crested and pelagic cormorants build big stick nests on the rocks and precariously cling to the steep sides. They fish the waters below the cliffs, then fly up to the nests to regurgitate food for their chicks. It is the most heavily populated of some 76 cormorant colonies in the Vancouver Island area.

It is also in the top ten of 150 nesting areas for glaucous-winged gulls in the same Vancouver Island region, having more than 1,000 nesting pairs. Glaucous-winged gulls are the only B.C. gull species to nest on the coast. With about 150 pairs, Mandarte also has the densest population of song sparrows in North America. A hundred pairs of pigeon guillemots also nest on the island.

Paddlers beneath the cliffs may see graying, guano-encrusted viewing blinds, where devoted scientists spend hour upon hour, spying on the birds, inhaling the fowl air. They live in small cabins on the opposite side of the island. Studies of Mandarte's prolific bird life began in the late 1950s, and it is said that the island has produced more PhDs per acre than any other real estate in B.C.

The birds of Mandarte, however, have been of service to humans much longer. For nearly 200 years before scientists discovered the island, Indians of Saanich Peninsula's Tsawout and Tsaykum bands gathered gulls' eggs and camas bulbs from Mandarte every summer. By watching the moon and the tides, they knew when the eggs would be fresh. Only dull eggs would be taken because shiny ones were too old, so enough were always left to hatch. Cormorant eggs were never taken, although the odd cormorant made a fine family feast.

184

According to Indian legend, Mandarte was the child of Spieden, a woman who escaped from a monster on the mainland and became the first person to settle in the islands. The legend says Mandarte was swept away by the tide immediately after birth and Spieden called for help to Sidney Island. Sidney Island thrust out its long arm and caught the drifting child, and that's how Sidney Spit was formed.

D'Arcy Island — From Leper Colony to Park

Launching: Island View Beach; James Island wharf. *Hazards:* high winds in Haro Strait. *Drinking water:* not available.

D'Arcy Island, an 84-hectare provincial marine park at the north end of Haro Strait, doesn't get much use. Anchorage for yachts is poor and the most direct route for paddlers is a three-mile crossing from Island View Beach in the open waters of Haro Strait. The island is nonetheless a pleasant place, with a few gravel beaches, dense woods, and some small grassy areas for camping. Several wildflower species bloom on D'Arcy Island during spring and summer. From the south end of the island there are good views down Haro Strait to Gordon Head, Ten Mile Point, and Chatham and Discovery islands.

From Island View Beach the safest way to get there is not across the three-mile channel directly off the beach, but along a route of slightly more than five miles. Paddle north from Island View, then east across Cordova Channel to the south end of James Island. Follow the south shore of James Island, then cross Sidney Channel to Sidney Island. Follow Sidney Island's western shore to the south end of the island, then cross Hughes Passage to the north shore of D'Arcy Island.

The best way to find good campsites on D'Arcy is simply to circumnavigate it, a total of two miles. One of the nicest, and largest, beaches is on the east side, facing Little D'Arcy Island, which is privately owned. Little D'Arcy has some small, pleasant beaches which belong to the public. Above the beach on D'Arcy is a grass-covered campsite with room for three or four tents.

The forest on the island is virtually impenetrable, with no trails. Most beaches are rocky, with lots of driftwood logs piled against the edge of the forest. Beachcombers who walk the perimeter of the island at low tides often see small brownish raccoons foraging along the shores.

Fishing around the reefs off the south end of the island, and between D'Arcy and Little D'Arcy, can be good for cod. Snorkelling is good here too. Paddling around Little D'Arcy and into a narrow natural harbour is fun.

D'Arcy has a rather sordid past as a leper colony. From 1892 until 1924, lepers were marooned on the island and given supplies every three months. Many tried to escape on makeshift rafts and boats, but few survived. There were plans to run it as a prison, but instead it was taken over by the provincial government in 1958 and established as a marine park in 1967.

James Island, en route to D'Arcy, is well worth a stop, or a trip on its own. Although the island is privately owned, the beaches, which rival those on Sidney Island, belong to everyone. The island totals about 300

James Island.

hectares, and all of the 11-kilometre shoreline is sandy beach. At low tides you can walk around the entire island in bare feet.

For more than 70 years the public was deprived of the beaches on James Island, because of the dangers associated with an explosives factory. Canadian Industries Limited, who owned the island from 1913 to 1987, had a foreshore lease which gave them jurisdiction down to low water, prohibiting the public from landing. By 1915, when CIL got British contracts for explosives, 800 men, most of whom lived on the island with their families, were employed in the island's TNT plant. During World War I, 16 million kilograms of TNT from James Island were shipped to Allied Forces. It was explosives from James Island that were aboard the French ship *Mont Blanc* when it blew up in Halifax Harbour in 1917, killing 1,654 people.

The explosives plant on James Island shut down in 1978, but for some unknown reason, the company continued to enjoy the benefit of a foreshore lease that gave virtual ownership of the beaches. When the lease came up for renewal in 1986, however, it was not renewed, and the beaches were returned to their rightful owners — the public. If you visit James Island today, remember the land above the high-tide line is private, but the beaches are yours.

Discovery Island — Where Two Straits Meet

Launching: Cattle Point; ramp on Beach Drive just north of Oak Bay Marina. *Hazards:* strong south winds from Juan de Fuca Strait; tides up to three knots in Baynes Channel, up to five knots in Plumper Passage. *Drinking water:* not available.

Discovery Island, off the shores of Victoria's Oak Bay district, lies at the meeting place of Haro and Juan de Fuca straits. During winter it is frequently battered by south winds funnelling up Juan de Fuca: much of the vegetation at the south end of the island stands as mute testimony of the fierceness of the storms. The branches of stunted evergreens cringe away from the sea, appearing even on a still day as though they're standing in a howling gale. Logs and flotsam are piled high up the shore and occasionally hikers find driftwood in fields far above the high-tide line.

From Cattle Point, where there are two large boat ramps, Discovery Island lies two nautical miles due east. This is treacherous water, with strong tides and frequent winds, and the trip should not be undertaken by inexperienced paddlers. Paddlers should make this crossing only on days of guaranteed calm. It's almost a mile and a half across Baynes Channel to the nearest point of land, in the Chatham Islands group. From here there are several choices through a maze of waterways, islands and islets. This is terrific paddling territory, but the Chatham Islands and the north side of Discovery are Indian land and therefore private.

Discovery Island Provincial Marine Park, a total of 61 hectares, encompasses about two-thirds of the island, on the south side. It was donated to the people of British Columbia by Captain E.G. Beaumont, who died in 1967 after living on Discovery for nearly half a century. A generous man, Capt. Beaumont ferried boy scouts and sea cadets back and forth on his boat, the *Discovery Isle*, for summer camping trips. He also donated the land for Beaumont Marine Park on North Pender, and for Beaumont Park at Fraser Lake, in the B.C. interior.

Much of the upland above the beaches is open grass fields. Camas, broom and other wild plants bloom here. There are places to camp and a few crude trails along the shores and through the forests. One service road leads to a lighthouse on Sea Bird Point, established in 1886. The point is named for an American paddle steamer which burned off the point in 1858. Gravel beaches, lined with logs, are small but plentiful. Salmon fishing in Plumper Passage, particularly off the mouth of the channel between Discovery and the Chatham Islands, is often excellent. The real draw here, however, is the paddling — with so many reefs and islets, channels, lagoons and salt marshes, you could spend a whole weekend poking around.

West of Discovery Island, between the island and Gonzales Point, are the Chain Islets. These are a fascinating stop for bird watchers in summer, when about 3,500 glaucous-winged gulls, 370 pelagic cormorants, and 60 pigeon guillemots are nesting. The islets are part of a 170-hectare ecological reserve, established in 1979 to protect the birds as well as the wildflowers and marine life. You can't land here, but you can paddle around the islets.

Discovery Island.

Other Books of Interest

Here are some other books for Gulf Islands explorers.

The Coast of British Columbia. Rosemary Neering. Whitecap Books Ltd., North Vancouver, B.C., 1989.

Cruising Guide to British Columbia, Volume I The Gulf Islands. Bill Wolferstan. Whitecap Books Ltd., North Vancouver, B.C., updated 1987.

An Explorer's Guide: Marine Parks of British Columbia. Peter Chettleburgh. Heritage House Publishing, Surrey, B.C., 1985.

A Gulf Islands Patchwork. Published for the Gulf Islands Branch of the B.C. Historical Association, Victoria, B.C., 1961.

Mayne Island and the Outer Gulf Islands, A History. Marie Elliott. Gulf Islands Press, Mayne Island, 1984.

Salt Spring Island. Bea Hamilton. Mitchell Press Ltd., Vancouver, B.C., 1969.

Snapshots of Early Salt Spring and Other Favoured Islands. Collected by Richard Mouat Toynbee and Other Kindred Souls. Mouat's Trading Co. Ltd., Ganges, B.C., 1978.

About the Author

Bruce Obee is a Vancouver Island writer who specializes in outdoors, travel and environmental topics. He began a freelance career in 1977 after five years in the news business as a reporter for *Victoria Times*, editor of the *Sidney Review*, and staff correspondent for the Canadian Press in Victoria. His articles are published by *Canadian Geographic*, *Beautiful British Columbia*, *Travel&Leisure*, the *New York Times*, *Nature Canada*, *BC Outdoors*, *Alfred Hitchcock's Mystery Magazine*, and others. Some of his writing is published in high-school and university textbooks.

He is winner of the Tourism British Columbia Travel Writers Award, and the Western Magazine Award for writing in the outdoors/recreation field.

An avid canoeist, bicyclist, hiker and boater, he lives in Deep Cove, on Saanich Peninsula, with his wife, Janet Barwell-Clarke, a biologist, and his daughters, Nicole and Lauren.